ALVESTON
THROUGH TIME
Rosemary King

AMBERLEY PUBLISHING

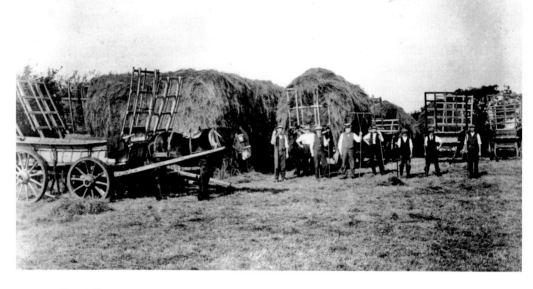

Hay Hauling at Vilner Hill Alveston on 23⁴ October 1931.

Hay Hauling, Vilner
This seems to be very late for bringing in hay, October 1931. Was it a very bad summer? The gentleman in the boater hat is H. G. Bush, nephew of Edward, who succeeded him at The Grove in 1908 when Edward died. The other gentlemen are his farm workers.

First published 2009

Amberley Publishing Plc
Cirencester Road, Chalford,
Stroud, Gloucestershire, GL6 8PE

www.amberley-books.com

Copyright © Rosemary King, 2009

The right of Rosemary King to be identified as the
Author of this work has been asserted in accordance
with the Copyrights, Designs and Patents Act 1988.

ISBN 978 1 84868 180 4

British Library Cataloguing in Publication Data.
A catalogue record for this book is available from
the British Library.

Typeset in 9.5pt on 12pt Celeste.
Typesetting by Amberley Publishing.
Printed in the UK.

Introduction

Alveston parish, which includes Rudgeway and Earthcott or Herdicot as it was once known, is situated around the Ridgeway between Bristol and Gloucester. Earthcott on the eastern slope away from the river Severn, and Alveston the newer village clusters to the west. Part of Rudgeway was originally in Olveston parish but boundary changes over the years have given Grovesend to Thornbury, and allocated all of Rudgeway now to Alveston plus the housing developments along the Stroud, which include Wolfridge and Lime Grove. The old church at Rudgeway was a 'Chapel of Ease' of Olveston church until 1846 when Alveston became a separate parish.

In 1994 Alveston Parish Council under the chairmanship of the late John Dyer, decided to hold an exhibition of photographs to show the changing face of the village over the past 100 years since Parish Councils had taken the place of the old Vestry Committees. At that time my husband John was a Parish Councillor, and he was asked to organise this. A request was made for anyone with old photographs to lend them for copying, and a friend Dr. L. G. Bray a former teacher at Thornbury G rammar School under took the task.

Before this in 1957 Alveston Women's Institute had won first prize with Birdlip W.I. in a competition organised by the Local History Committee of the Gloucestershire Community Council, for *Village History within Living Memory*, and to mark the fortieth anniversary of the W.I. in 1959 the book was printed. Owing to the cost of printing at that time pictures were not included, this year marks the ninetieth anniversary of the Women's Institute, and some of those original pictures are in this new book.

Our grateful thanks to all those people who gave and lent us photographs.

ALVESTON NATIONAL SCHOOL,

FOR THE

Education of the Poor

In the Principles of the Established Church.

Rules for the guidance of Parents.

1.—Children will be admitted every Monday Afternoon, at Two o'clock, by the Minister of the Parish, or by a Member of the Committee, when one of the Parents will be expected to attend and promise obedience to the Rules.

2.—They must send their Children regularly to School, with their hair cut short, clean washed and combed, and with their clothes well mended, at a Quarter to Nine in the Morning, and a Quarter to Two in the Afternoon.

Take Notice.—Unless you enforce your Children's regular attendance, no good can come to you, the Child, or the School.

3.—That on Sundays, Christmas Day, Good Friday, and the Days of National Fast and Thanksgiving, they shall send their Children to the School punctually at a Quarter to Nine in the Morning, and at a Quarter before Two in the Afternoon, or at such other hours as shall be directed by the Master, before they proceed to Church.

4.—In no case is a Child to be absent without a Ticket of Leave : but in case of Sickness, or any accident befalling a Child, immediate Notice must be sent to the Master : in default of which the Child will be suspended (that is, will not be permitted to attend the School) until one of the Parents appears before the Visitor, and will then be finally expelled, unless a satisfactory explanation be given.

5.—That no Parents be permitted to take their Children out of the School, without appearing before the General Committee, or Visitors, and assigning their reason.

6.—Parents, on the admittance of their Child, will be required to pay 6d. for the use of the Books ; and they are to send Two-pence every Monday Morning for the Child's Schooling.

N.B.—Children who may be absent after having been once entered in the Books, must pay the customary Two-pence a Week as if they were present.

7.—That they direct their Children to pay strict attention to the following Rules.

Rules for the Children.

1.—They must go to and from School in an orderly manner.

2.—They must behave respectfully to their Teachers, and strictly obey the directions given them.

3.—They must take the greatest care of their Books, Slates, &c.

4.—They must be diligent whilst at School, and behave with the greatest reverence during Prayers there, and in the time of Divine Service at Church.

5.—They must be kind one to another, never quarrel, never tell a lie, cheat, steal, nor swear, nor be guilty of any indecent behaviour.

CADDELL HOLDER,

CURATE OF ALVESTON.

Alveston National School, August, 1836.

Gutch and Martin, Printers, Small-Street, Bristol.

Original rules of 1836.

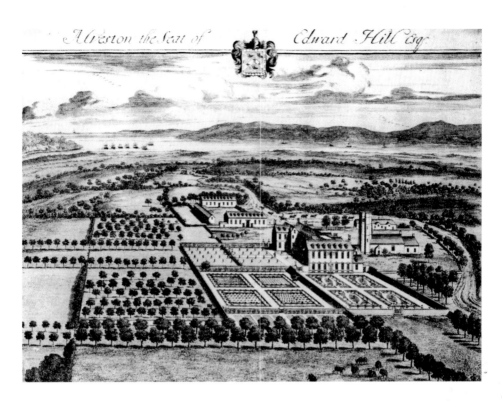

Church Farm

The Kip's engraving entitled 'Alveston the Seat of Edward Hill Esq' is believed to represent the planned or existing building of 1712. The present Church Farm is all that now remains of that building. Edward was the great grandson of Colonel Thomas Veele, whose father Nicholas purchased the Manor in the late 1500s. By the time Bristol Siddeley purchased the house in the 1960s, part was being used to store farm machinery etc., and it was in a bad state of repair. It was later purchased by Rolls-Royce as a guest house for overseas visitors.

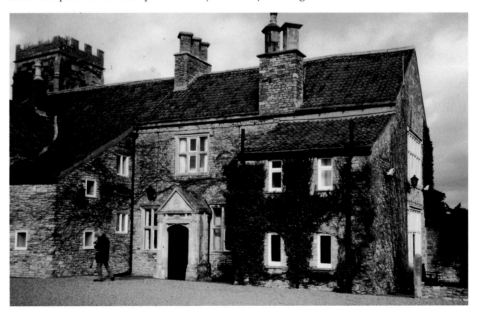

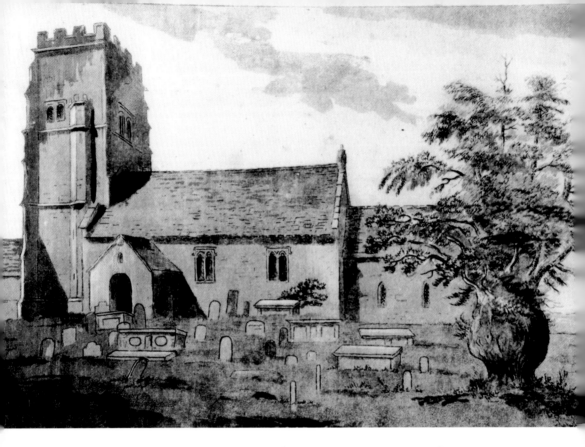

Old Church at St Helens

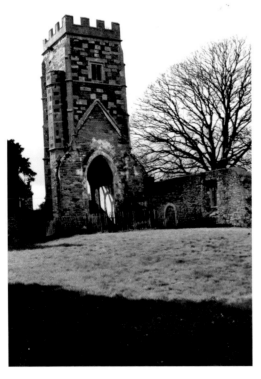

The site of the old church of St. Helens is documented from 1106. Also purchased by Rolls Royce in 1960, it was built on what was reputed to be a round pagan site, containing wall paintings from the fourteenth century and earlier. There were also drawings of two ships on the porch wall which the National Maritime Museum have judged to date from between 1650 and 1700. Only a part of the fourteenth century tower and the remains of some tombstones are still to be seen.

Colonel Thomas Veele
A supporter of the Royalist
cause in the Civil War, at
the outbreak he was in
command of the trainbands
of the Berkeley Division
in Gloucestershire, and in
1644 held Berkeley Castle
for the King. Thomas fled
the country with the King,
returning in 1660, he died in
1663, and was buried under
the chancel in the family
vault. In 1960 when the
builders were demolishing
the roof timbers, one man
jumped down onto the stone
slab which covered the grave,
and fell in with the skeletons!
Hobart Bird's book on *Old
Gloucestershire Churches*
mentions a Norman doorway,
with early type chevron
ornament on the arch, and
possible Saxon work.

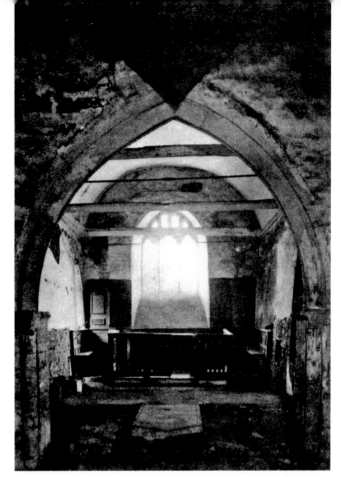

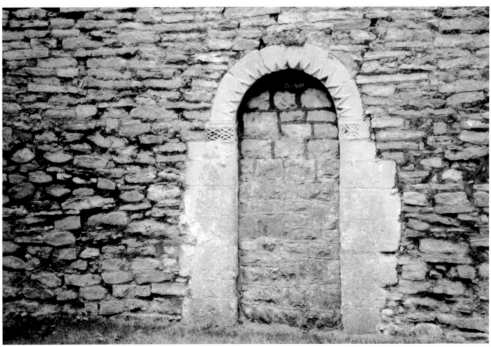

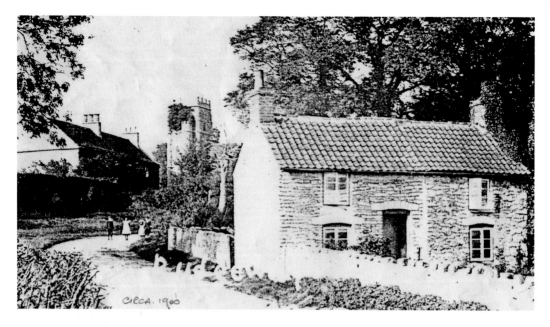

Old Turnpike House

When the Turnpike Trust undertook to maintain a section of road, a separate act had to be passed, previously each Parish had been responsible for the upkeep of its roads and this meant that many were in a bad state of repair. Turnpike cottage is not now on the main road, it having been realigned over the years, and the cottage itself extended. On the 1841 Census Edward Biddle is living here with his wife and seven children, he had previously been 'pike keeper' at Stone having paid £752 per annum for the priviledge.

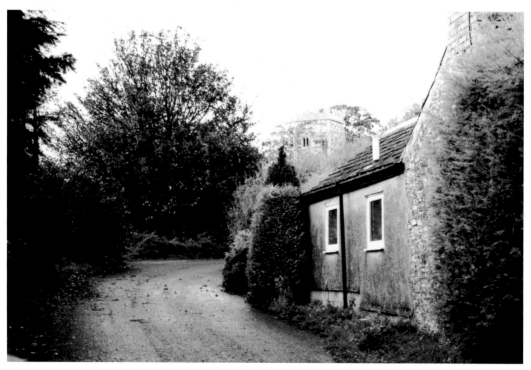

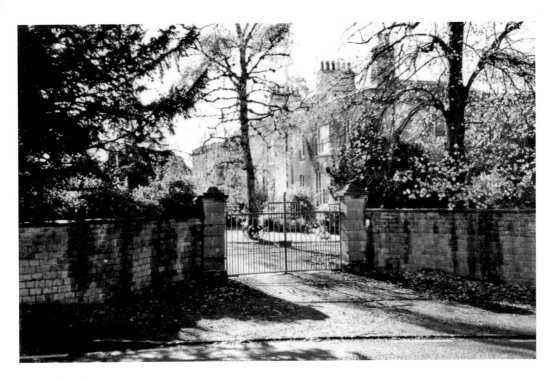

The Elms

Once a year Mr Gardiner of The Elms entertained the school children to a tea and prize giving. This picture was taken in 1916 as they all arrived dressed in their 'Sunday best'. The present Pypers replaced an older house in the grounds in the late 1700s. Over the years The Elms has been the home of many army and naval personnel, until it was purchased by Sir George Stanley White in 1938, grandson of the founder of the Bristol Aeroplane Co.

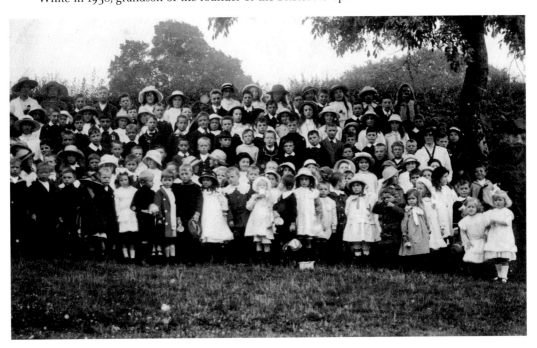

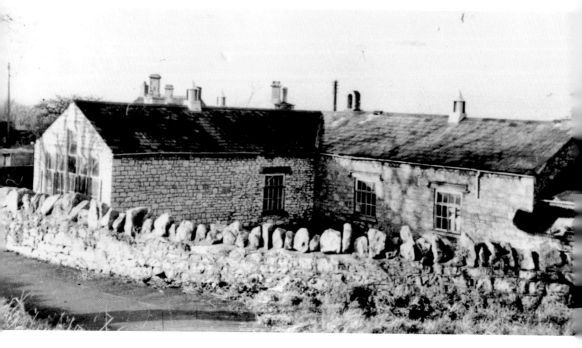

Alveston National School

Built in 1835, the first teacher was William Williams who had been an apprenticed carpenter. A few years later the school closed through lack of funds, but it reopened in 1845 with Miss Emily Lambert teaching on a salary of £12 per year. There was a proposal in 1871 to substantially enlarge the school, but instead an infants' school was built at Earthcott, and an extra classroom was built at Rudgeway. The school closed in 1965 and the children transferred to the new St. Helen's while at Rudgeway the buildings were converted to two houses in the 1970s. The extra classroom which was added in 1876 can still be seen at the rear.

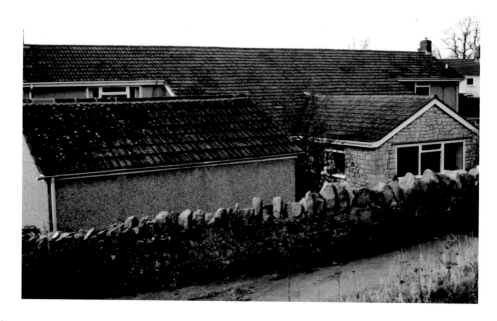

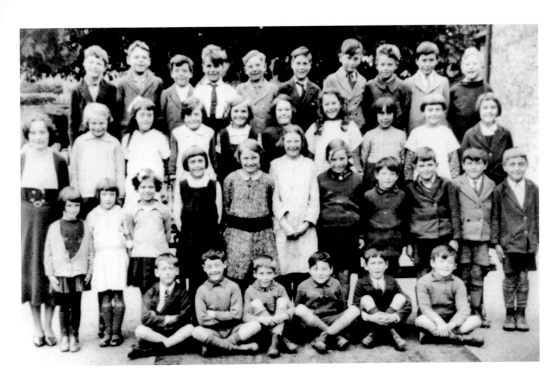

Old School at Rudgeway

Two pictures from the old school at Rudgeway, after the enlargement in 1876 there were still only three rooms. By the 1940s there were up to fifty children in a class sometimes sitting three to a desk. The toilets were outside and there was no room for games or P.E., but despite this an old ex-pupil and teacher said that the children were regarded as 'good at arithmetic' at the Thornbury Grammar School.

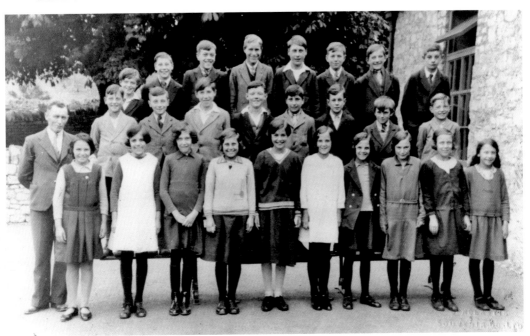

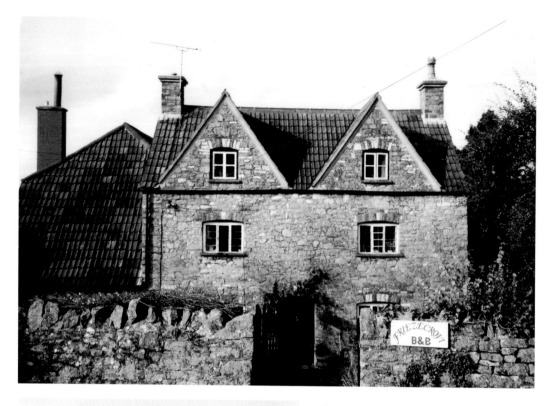

PARTICULARS

Delightful Freehold Eighteenth Century Gabled House with Outbuildings and Land

—— known as ——

"FRIEZECROFT," RUDGEWAY

in the parish of Olveston and containing an area of about

3 acres   2 roods   6 perches

THE HOUSE, which is stone built, has twin gables and tiled roof.

The Accommodation comprises—Passage, Two Sitting Rooms, Kitchen with stove, and large Store Room. On the First Floor are Two Bedroom and Two Bedrooms above.

THE OUTBUILDINGS which are in a walled in yard include stone and tiled Implement Shed, Two Loose Boxes, Pig Stye and Fowls House.

Certain of the Windows in the House are stone mullioned and there are some excellent oak beams in some of the rooms.

Company's Water and Electric Light pass the property.

The Property is Freehold and Free from Ground Rent.

VACANT POSSESSION will be given on completion.

Tithe Redemption Annuity 3s. 8d.

This Property is situated just off the main Bristol-Gloucester Road and commands superb views over the Severn Valley and the River Estuary. It lends itself to easy conversion as a charming small Country House within easy reach of Bristol and in the Berkeley Hunt.

There is a frequent Bus Service to Bristol and Thornbury.

The Land is of light loam and very productive.

Such Estate as the Vendor has power to convey in Ord. No. 652 is included in the sale but subject to any existing rights of the public or individuals.

Friezecroft

A diarist of 1845 names William Irons as the former occupier of Friezecroft, followed by William Withers as tenant when it was owned by Mr Peach of Tockington, and in Olveston Parish. It was bought for his own occupation by Roy Luce the Thornbury auctioneer in the 1940s for £2020.

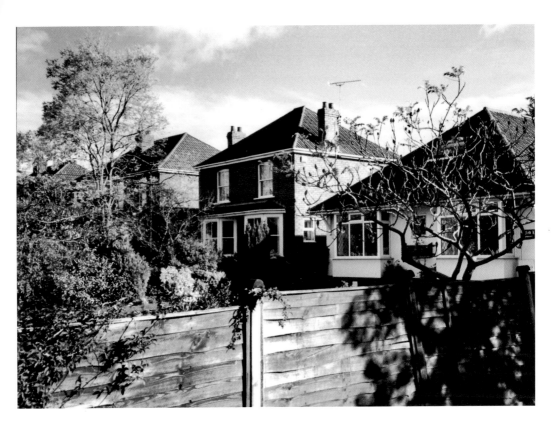

The Red Lodge

Mrs Mills and her friend and lodger Miss Pater sitting outside the Red Lodge. Mrs Mills owned the land which became Rudgeway Park and carried on the business of 'market gardener' here for many years taking her produce to a stall in Bristol Market.

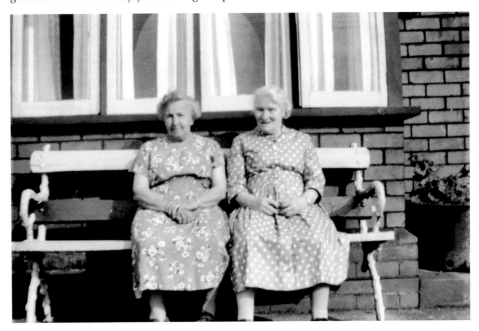

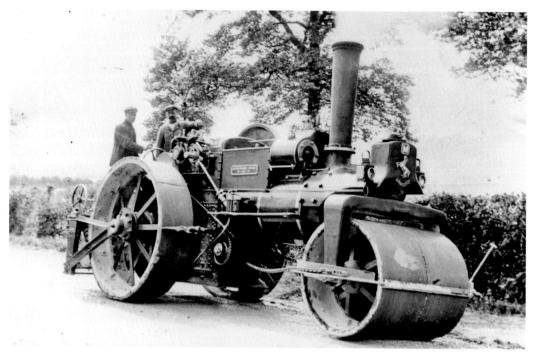

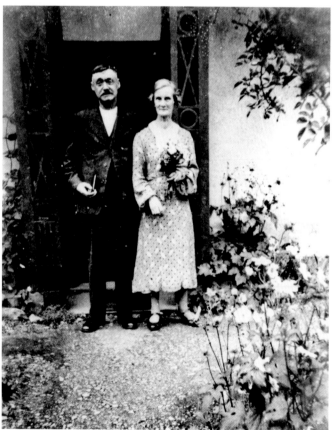

Frank Lippiatt

Frank Lippiatt drove the county steamroller in the early 1900s. Before he married he would ride his bicycle to Gloucester at the weekend from his home then in Tockington to see his fiancée Miss Emily Need. On Monday morning he would send her a post card to say that he had arrived home safely, and mark it with a cross to show where he would be working that week. At this time a reply could be sent to him c/o Head-County Steamroller, and the name of the village.

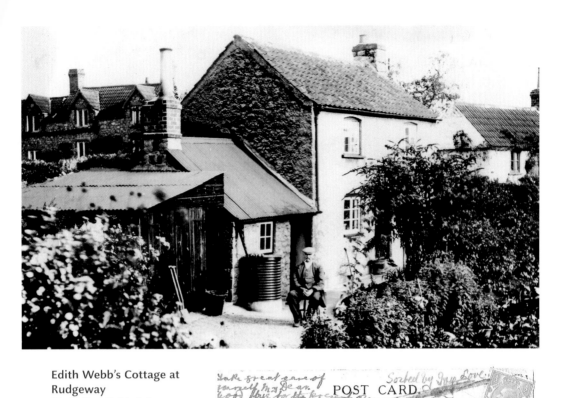

Edith Webb's Cottage at Rudgeway

Mr C. Barnfield sitting outside Reginald and Edith Webb's cottage at Rudgeway. In 2008 a postcard was discovered sent by Reginald Webb from Verdun to his wife when he was serving in the First World War, where he received the D.C.M. Returning safely, he completed fifty years service with the Electricity Board by 1954 when he was awarded a long service medal.

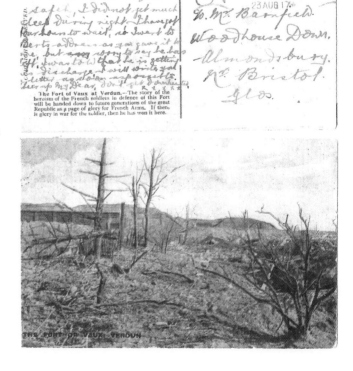

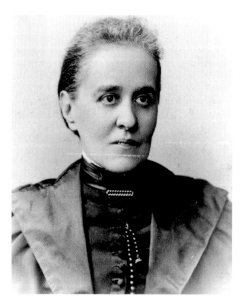
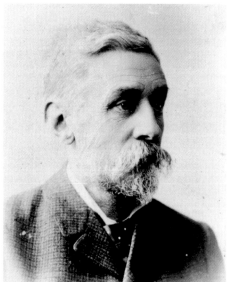

Silverhill

Mary Frances (Bush) and William Alford Ward married in 1883, and lived at Silverhill then called Fernhill. The house was built by John Ward William's grandfather in 1810, and lived in by various family members until 1930 when it became an hotel and country club. During the Second World War it was used for a time as a convalescent home. In the 1950s the name was changed to Silverhill, the name of the field on which it stands, and a school was run here by Mrs Wadsworth. In 1994, the school moved to Winterbourne where they had another establishment, and the house was acquired by Wyman Harris Research.

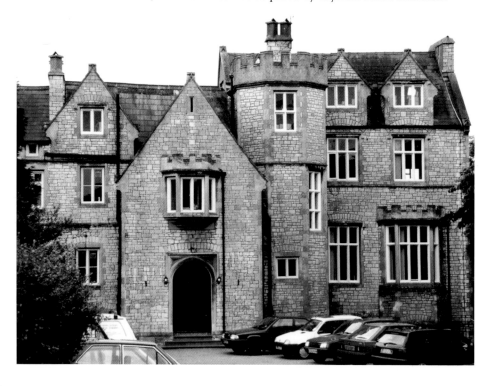

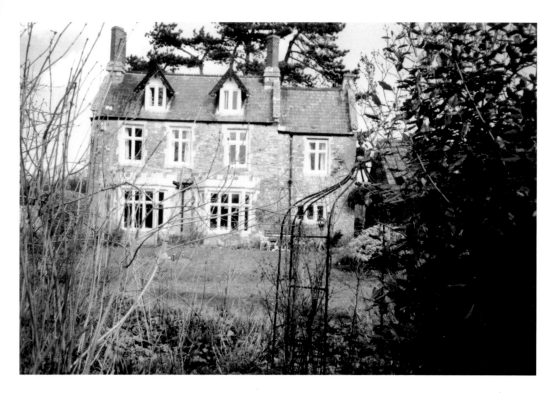

Oak Lodge

First mentioned in the deeds of Elberton Manor in 1713, the house is marked but not named on Isaac Taylor's map of 1777. Formerly known as the Royal Oak, Tockington, it was listed in *Patterson's Roads* of 1828, and was a staging post for the coaches to and from the Aust Ferry. It was owned by John Ward before he built the house opposite, then known as Tockington Hill House, now Silverhill.

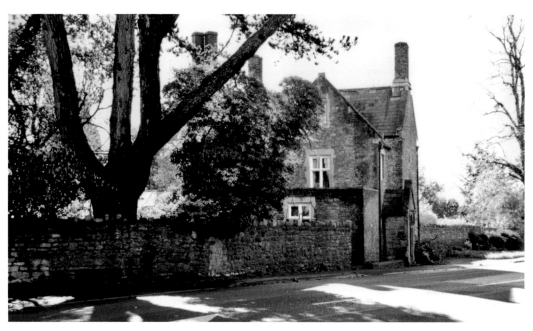

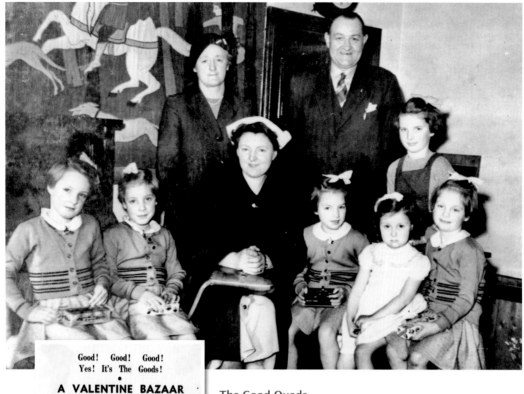

The Good Quads

A Bazaar at the Jubilee Hall in 1955 was opened by Mrs Good and her daughters who were quads. Children of multiple births didn't usually survive and so the quads were famous. Also in the picture are Mrs Haddrell, and Jack Thompson, who was chairman of Alveston Parish Council at that time, and had a bakery in the single-storey building below.

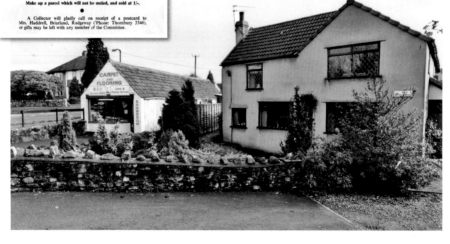

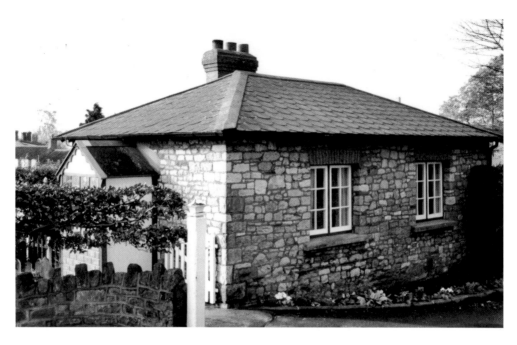

The Friezewood Estate

In 1844 the Friezewood estate was bought by Thornbury solicitor Thomas Crossman, the old house of the Dyer family having been already pulled down, and a new house was built, with a lodge. The house was in Olveston Parish, and the lodge in Alveston, as the parish boundary at that time ran along the side of the Ridgway. Thomas Crossman's son Edward founded Hambrook Village Hospital in 1867, his son Francis following him as Hon. Medical Director. Mr T. P. Rogers was another prominent owner of the house and a former president of The Society of Merchant Venturers.

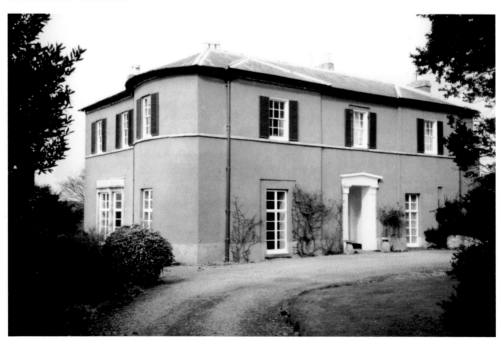

BRISTOL to BIRMINGHAM, BY GLOUCESTER, TEWKESBURY,
WORCESTER, DROITWICH, AND BROMSGROVE, CONTINUED TO SHEFFIELD, BY SUTTON COLDFIELD, LICHFIELD, BURTON UPON TRENT, DERBY, AND CHESTERFIELD.

	From Sheffield	From * BRISTOL, Gloucestershire, to	From Bristol	
FILTON. Pen Park, ——.	162			
ALMONDSBURY, before, Knowle, *George Gibbs,* Esq.; and farther to the left, Over Court, *John Vaughan,* Esq.; beyond Almondsbury, a most beautiful view of the river Severn, at a distance, and the hills beyond it.	159¾	Horfield	2¼	HORFIELD. Stoke Gifford Park, Dowager Duchess of *Beaufort.*
	158¼	Filton	3¾	
	156	Patchway Green	6	
	155	Almondsbury	7	ROYAL OAK. Tockington; *Samuel Peach Peach,* Esq.
		A little farther, 🖙 *to Aust Passage Inn 5 m.*		
ALVESTON. *W. N. Tonge,* Esq.; and at Thornbury, the ruins of the Castle.	153½	Royal Oak	8½	
	152¾	Alveston	9¼	FALFIELD, near, Tortworth Cottage, Hon. Col. *Moreton;* and Tortworth Vicarage, Rev.
FALFIELD. Hill Court, Miss *Fust.*		*To Chipping Sodbury 7½ m.* 🖙		Dr. *Cooke;* near which is Cromhall Park, ——.
	151¾	Ship Inn	10¼	
BERKELEY HEATH. At Berkeley, The Castle, Col. *Berkeley.*		🖙 *to Thornbury 1 m.* *Bristol to THORNBURY* 11¼ *m.*		

The Royal Oak

Patterson's Roads, printed in 1828, lists the Royal Oak at Alveston and the Royal Oak, Tockington, opposite Silverhill. By 1835, Richard Meredith was innkeeper at the Royal Oak. By the 1880s the Royal Oak was a farmhouse, and Luke Watkins was tenant, and by 1935 ownership had passed to Mr Henry Wilmot. A galvanised iron manufacturer born in Bristol, Henry's parents had built the chalet at the top of Alveston Hill as a weekend home. In 1954 the house was bought by Thomas Silvey, owners of a coal and aggregates company from Bristol, and then in 1978 divided into two houses.

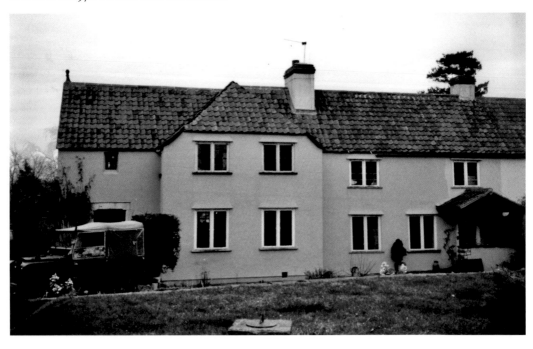

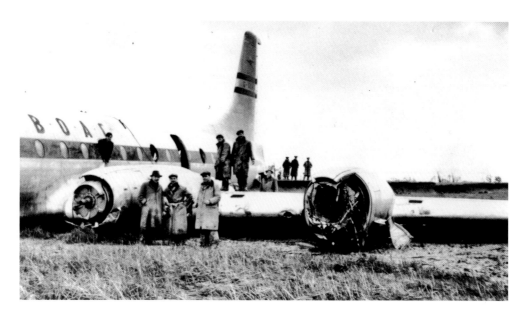

Bill Pegg

Also bought by Henry Wilmot who lived there while renovations were carried out across the road at Oak Farm was Hazelcote. Built by James Hawkins, father of the Thornbury builder Phillip, it was later purchased by Bill Pegg who went on to become the chief test pilot for the Bristol Aeroplane Co. He was test flying a Bristol Britannia aeroplane when he was forced to crash land at Littleton-upon-Severn. All the crew walked away unhurt, thanks to the soft mud, and the skill of the pilot.

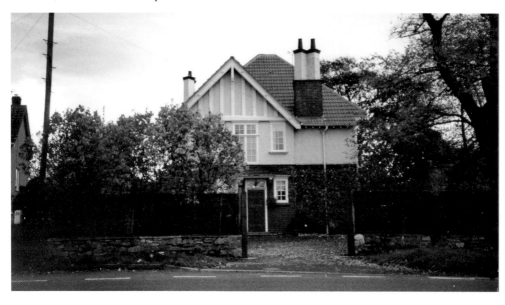

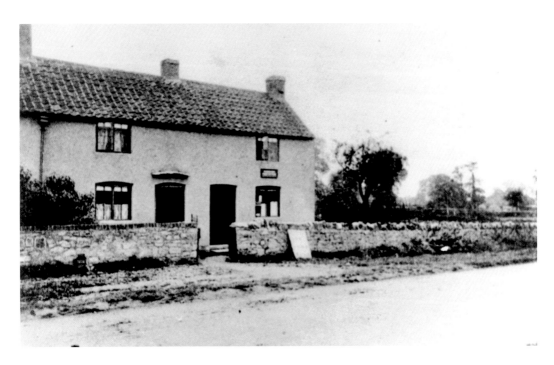

Rudgeway Post Office

Rudgeway has had two post offices on opposite sides of the road. The first was kept by Edward Biddle who had formerly lived at the Turnpike. In a book written about the post office and sub postmasters in 1899 by R. C. Tombs, it reads; 'A notable man in his day was Edward Biddle, on the Thornbury side of Bristol. Mr Biddle was sub postmaster at Rudgeway for over forty years, and occupied the post until his death in 1889 at the ripe old age of ninety-one years, when he was succeeded by his daughter, and she in turn, was succeeded by his son William Biddle who still holds the appointment.'

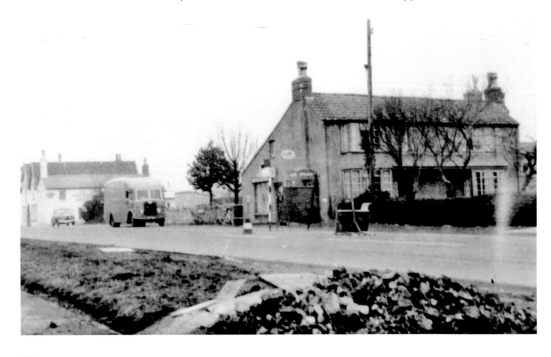

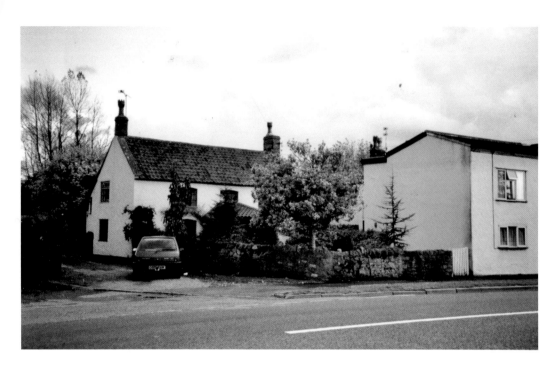

Masons Arms

Between 1851 and 1871 George Angel is listed as Musician and Beer Housekeeper, and lived with his wife Ann in the cottage next door to the present Masons Arms. Until about 1890 there was a blacksmith's shop next door which was incorporated into the present building, and can still be seen to the right of the picture. In 1881 Jacob Savery from Earthcott worked here. The Savery family had made the famous 'Savery Plough' which was exported to Canada and Australia until this village industry was taken over by the larger manufacturers.

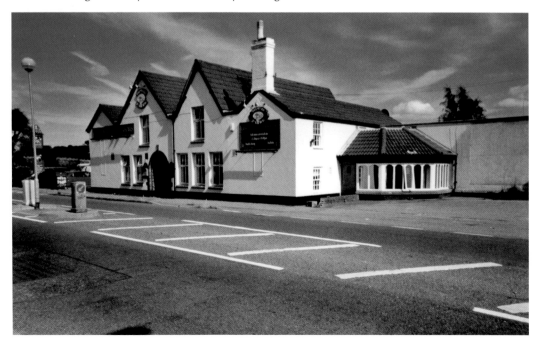

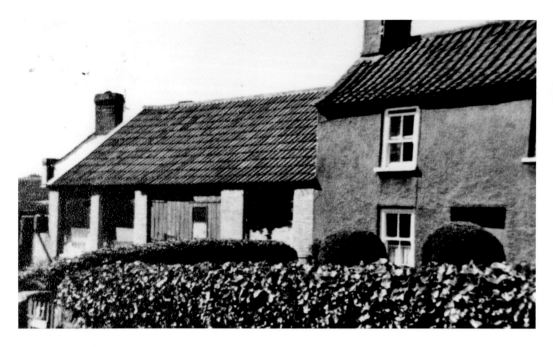

The Last Smithy

Jacob Savery had expanded the implement making business of his parents and grandparents at Earthcott into general agricultural sales. His uncle, Mark Savery, moved to a shop in Thornbury to do the same thing. When Jacob moved to Cheltenham, his smithy and shop were purchased by a brewery. The blacksmiths business meanwhile moved along the road to be run by Henry Smith, and later his son, Charles. The smithy closed in the 1950s and became a builder's yard, and later an annexe to the house.

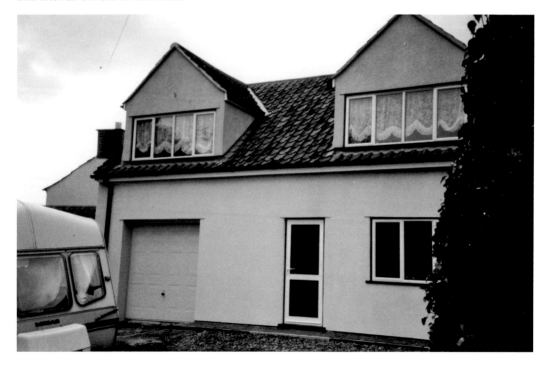

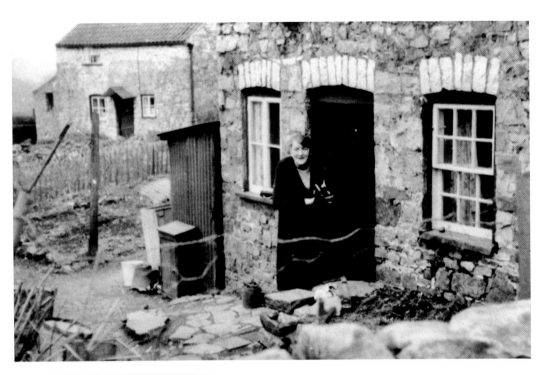

Alterations to the A38

In the 1960s alterations to the A38 were carried out and several cottages were demolished, the road was then straightened and raised in several places. Work in progress can be seen in the earlier picture of Rudgeway post office. Cottages between the post office and Hazelcote were demolished, and also several more houses opposite the Masons Arms, Vine Cottage where the Poole family lived (inset) and Mrs Moss (above), standing at the gate of her cottage which was due for demolition.

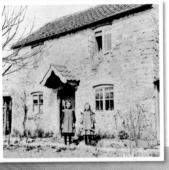

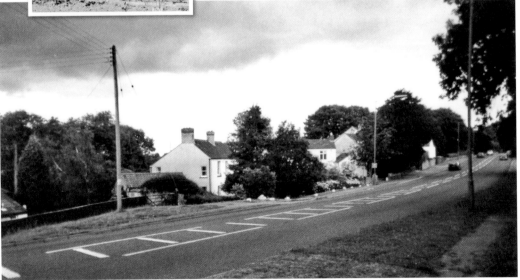

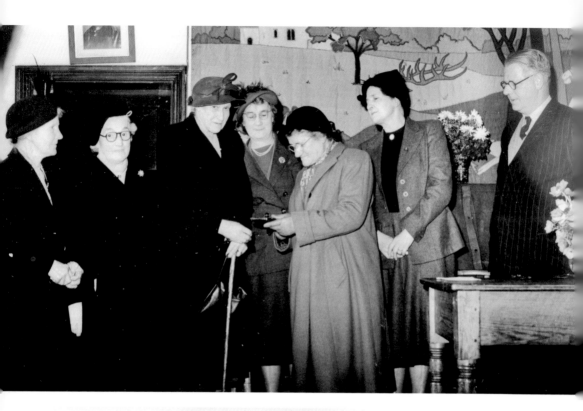

– A –
PUBLIC MEETING

WILL BE HELD AT THE

Jubilee Hall, Alveston,

ON

Saturday, 28th May, 1910

At 7.30 p.m.

to consider the question of providing a

Village Nurse for the Parish

and if considered desirable, to appoint a Committee to collect Subscriptions.

All Parishioners interested are invited to attend and to give in their names if willing to become Subscribers.

Unless sufficient support is promised it will be impossible to carry out the scheme.

BROWN, PRINTER, HIGH STREET, THORNBURY.

Nurse Baker

Another of the lost cottages was where Nurse Baker had lived. A public meeting was held at the Jubilee Hall in 1910 to consider the appointment of a village nurse. In the event one was not appointed until 1921, when the highly respected Nurse Baker was taken on. As there was no superannuation fund for District Nurses, the parishioners collected and presented her with a cheque in 1942. It was impossible to replace her however, and she continued to practice as a nurse until the early 1950s.

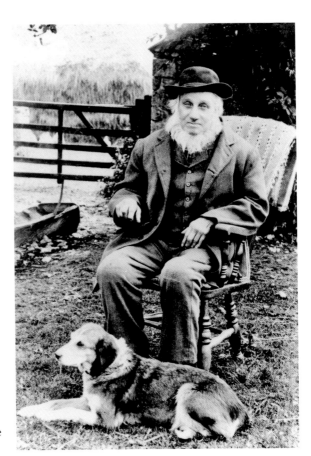

Forty Acre Farm

John Biddle (1827-1920) lived at Forty Acre Farm. He married Lucinda Harvey, and they had a total of sixteen children, some of whom are pictured with grandchildren. John was a founder member of Alveston Horticultural Society, and can be seen in a later picture wearing his medal. He was also one of the first parish councillors.

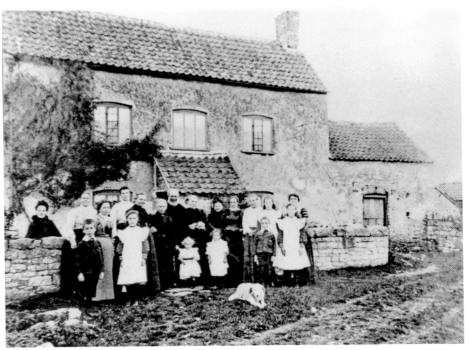

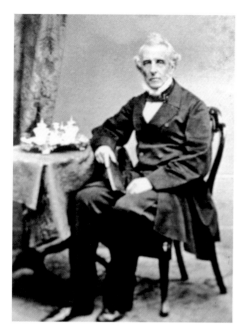
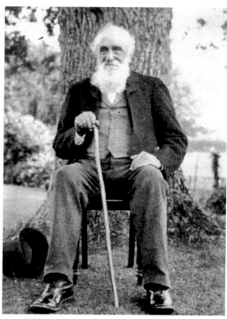

The Loans

The Loans, sometimes called The Lawns by Ordnance Survey on its 1881 map. William Bush married at Alveston in 1813 and purchased the Loans in the late 1700s, and his nephew John Whittington Bush lived here with his family for a number of years, until moving to Bath. Thomas inherited it in 1853 and lived there until his death in 1902. Purchased in the 1960s by Mr Hawkins, his widow has donated land for allotments to Alveston at a peppercorn rent in 2009.

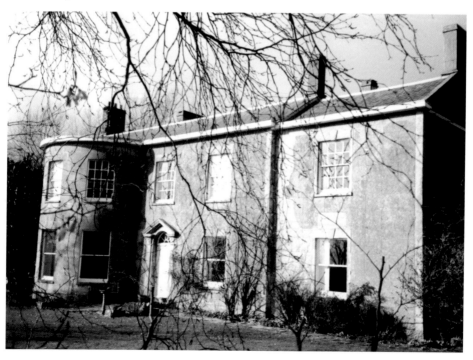

Church Cottages

(Right) Henry and Fanny Williams standing outside Church Cottages, Henry unfortunately lost an eye when breaking coal to stoke the church boiler.

(Inset) John Sage and his friend playing outside the cottages in the 1920s – the A38 had much less traffic then!

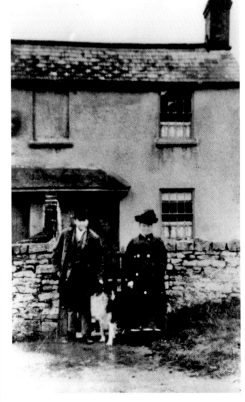

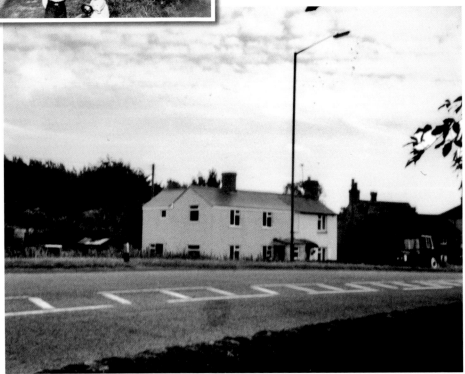

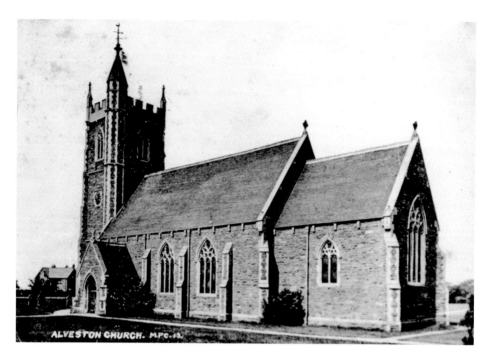

New Church

In 1885 a new church was built as the old one had become dilapidated and unsafe to use. The new site was nearer the large development of the village which had taken place since the 1839 Enclosure, a piece of land was given by Sir John Willoughby whose ancestors had held land in Alveston from the church for several hundred years. Edward and Thomas Bush gave £1230 each and other parishioners contributed to the £3675 total. Two bells were brought from the old church, as was the font.

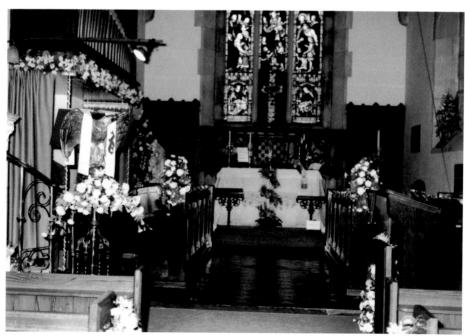

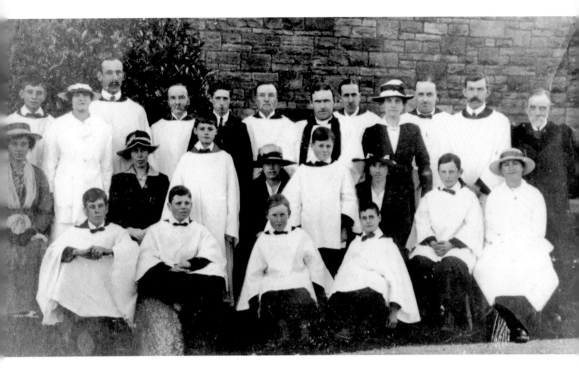

The Choir

Until 1846, Alveston had been a 'Chapel of Ease' of Olveston Church; it had no vicarage until 1897. The first occupant was Edward Langley, nephew of Thomas and Edward Bush, who can be seen to the right of the choir. The second choir picture dates from the 1960s. Charles Smith is fourth from the right in the back row; he sang with the choir for a total of seventy-five years.

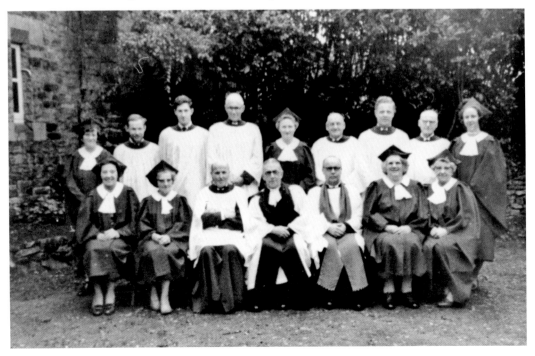

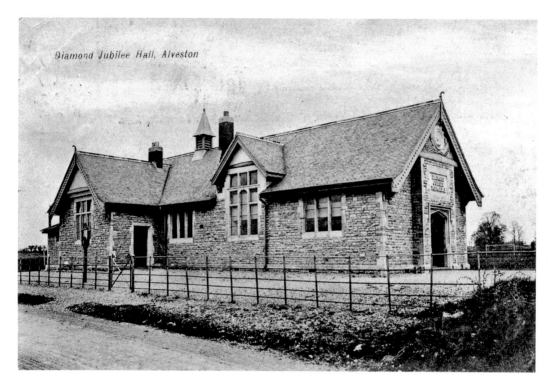

Diamond Jubilee Hall, Alveston

The Jubilee Hall

The Jubilee Hall was given to the village by Edward Bush to mark the Diamond Jubilee of Queen Victoria in 1897, together with the four acre field adjoining it. In 1938 Henry G. Bush donated the Lime Kiln Field. It was extended and a new entrance hall, kitchen and toilets were added in the 1980s which cover the original dedication.

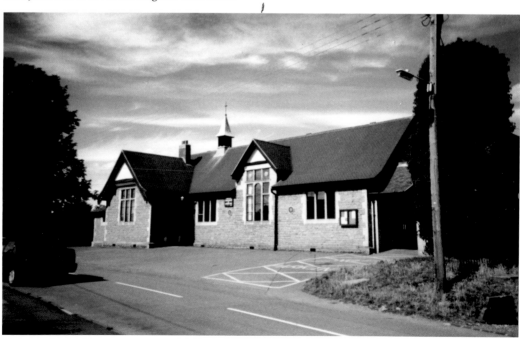

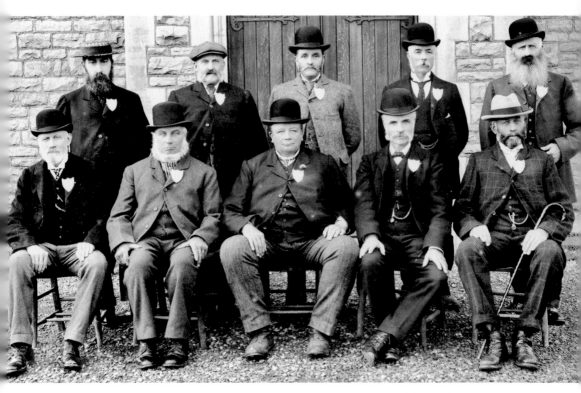

Alveston Horticultural Show

The hall has many uses. The gentlemen sitting outside in 1908 are the remaining committee members of the first Alveston Horticultural Show, wearing their medals for raising over £1000 for local medical charity. (Back row) J. W. Chambers, N. Lippiatt, F. Smith, T. Riddiford, C. Liddiatt. (Front row) G. Biddle, J. Biddle, T. Croome, G. Riddiford, L. Watkins.

The first show was held on the 'Timber Green' at Rudgeway. The later picture shows a poem written about it by Emma Riddiford being displayed in the 1960s. In 2009, the show was still being held, and was a great success.

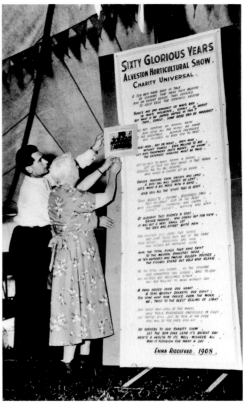

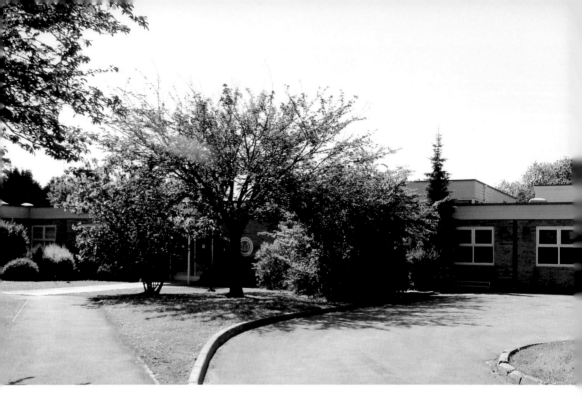

St Helens Primary School

St Helens Church of England Primary School opened on its new site next to the church in 1965. The children moved from the old school at Rudgeway and were thrilled to have light airy classrooms and a school field. The new headmaster was Mr C. B. Higgins.

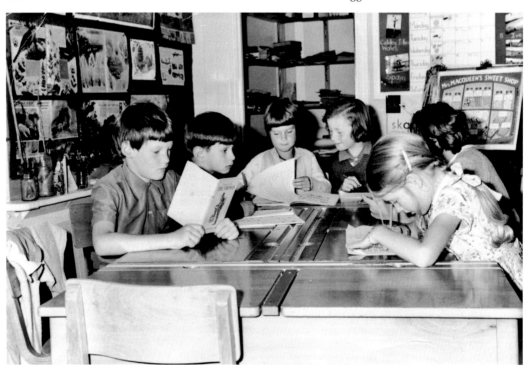

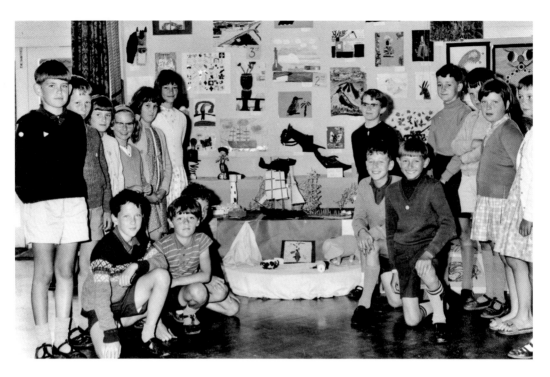

100 Years with Mrs Summers

The school had a hall where exhibitions of the children's work could be shown, this one in about 1966. To celebrate 100 years of the new church in 1985 the staff and children dressed in Victorian clothes. Mrs Charlotte Summers (back row, second left), a former teacher and granddaughter of John Biddle, planted a tree with headmaster Mr D. Griffiths.

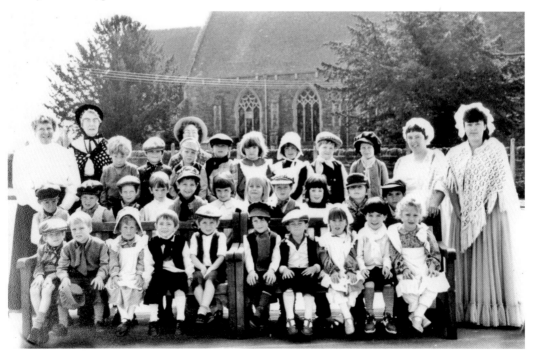

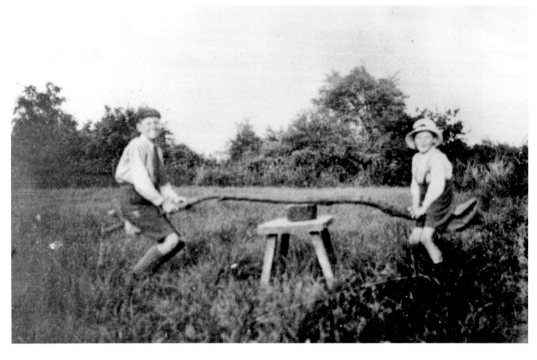

Bob and Dick Riddiford
Bob Riddiford and his brother Dick see-saw in the field where the Parish Council was to build new houses in 1920.

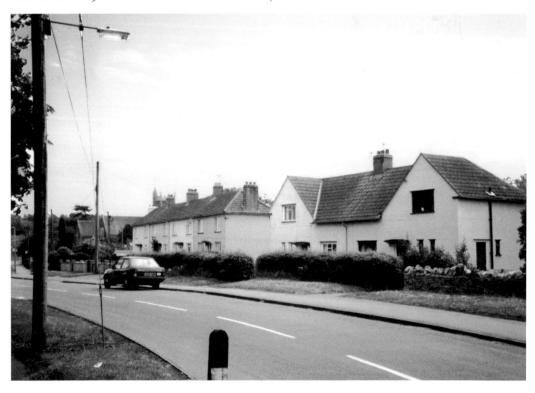

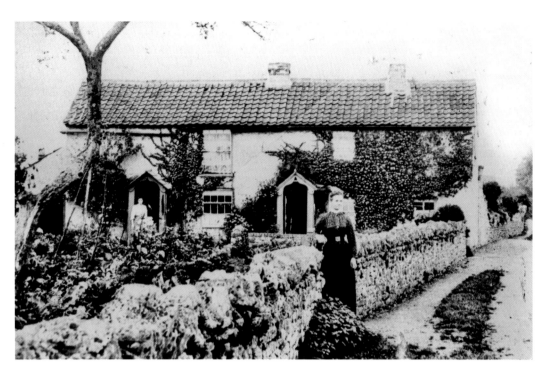

Greenhill Road

A cottage on Greenhill Road which was demolished to make an entrance for the bungalows for older residents in Underwood Close. Some of the large gardens of the original council houses were also used. Below you can see Mr Dyer, Mrs Bowyer and Mrs Webb 'digging for victory' in the 1940s!

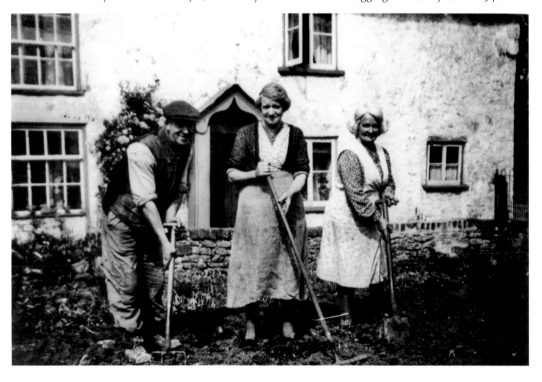

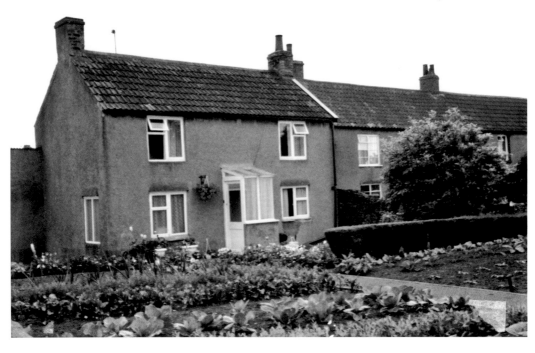

Greenhill 2009
The cottage on Greenhill which was developed in 2009 into two houses with double garages.

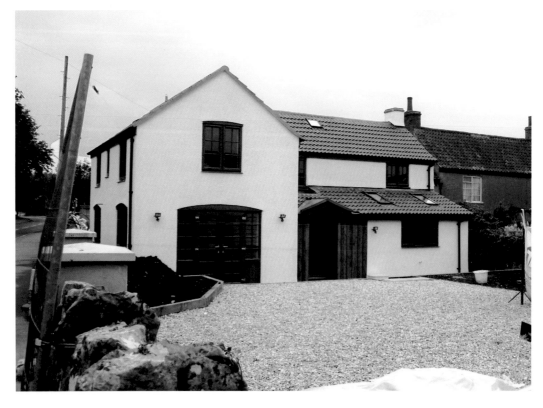

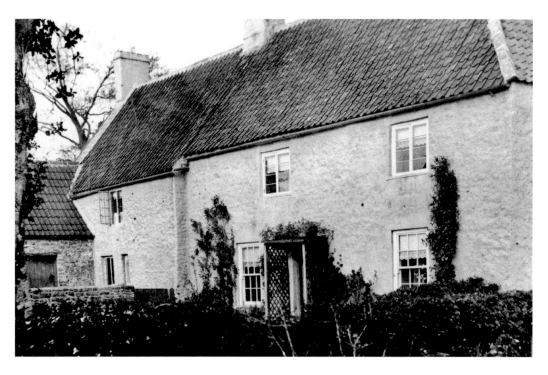

David's Lane Farmhouse

David's Lane Farm or earlier Raggs Farm, the first picture shows the house in 1939 when it was home to a Champion family. Listed in Linda Hall's *Book of Rural Houses*, it dates from the sixteenth century when it had a thatched roof and gables. Sale particulars of 1888 refer to it as Gunter's Farm (a former owner) with fifteen acres of land, which have all been built on over the years.

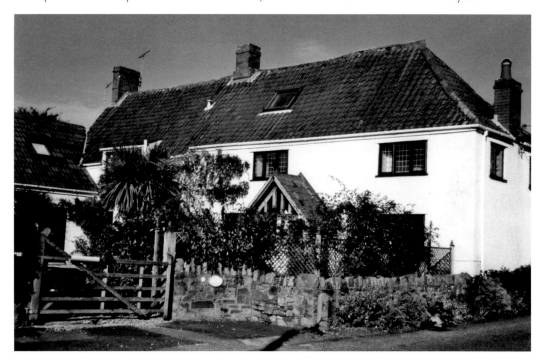

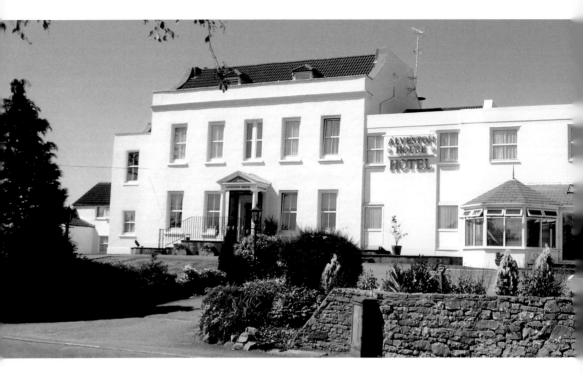

Alveston House Hotel

Alveston House was built by Edward Watkins Banker for his own use in the late eighteenth century. The house was rented by Thomas Helstone Esq who had a boarding and day school, and advertised 'the known salubrity of the air, the mild discipline of the school, and the extensive playgrounds'. A number of the children were aged fourteen to fifteen and had disabilities of varying degrees. Later residents have included Mr Lewis Jolly a Thornbury solicitor, and also in the 1930s Mr Barnwell designer for the Bristol Aeroplane Company. The house has also been used as a home for the elderly, and for the past forty years as an hotel.

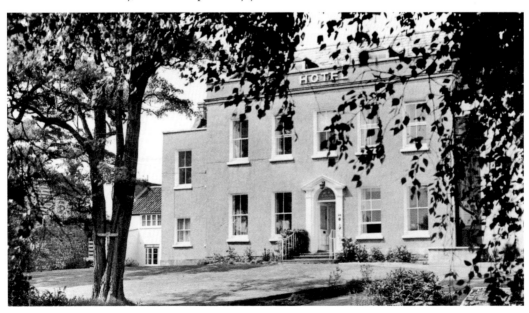

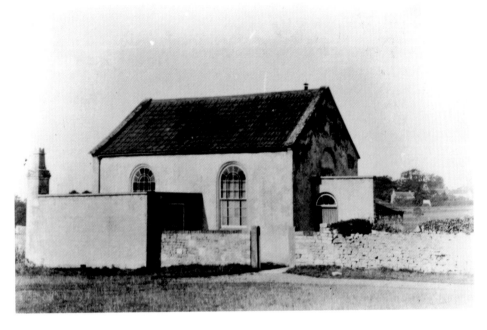

Methodist Chapel

Greenhill, originally common land, belonged by 1803 to William Cullimore of Earthcott, who donated a site for the chapel. This was completed in 1811, extensive renovations were carried out in 1892, but in 1964 a decision was made to build a new Methodist Chapel on the site, with entry off the new Wolfridge Ride road.

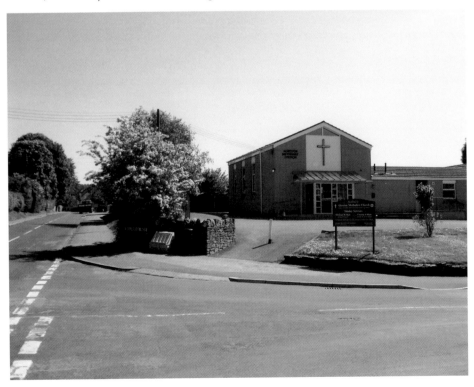

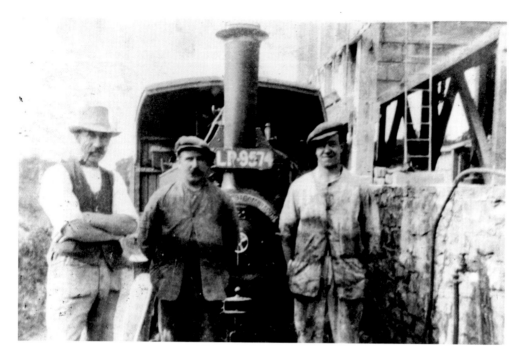

Greenhill Quarry

The quarry at Greenhill was developed by Samuel Stutchbury of the Firs, Alveston. He purchased the house and land known as Bodyces Farm in 1893. In 1908 the quarry was sold to the Teign Valley Granite Co., and then to Gloucester County Council. It closed in the 1930s. By the 1950s there was a proposal to use the old quarry as a refuse tip, but after opposition because of the amount of water it contained it was agreed that filling should only be of hard core. The 1957 W.I. Book notes that the water was 50-80ft deep at that time. *Inset:* Picture of the crusher taken about 1929; it was introduced after the 1914 war, was fed by hand, and it was dismantled when the quarry closed. The picture at the top shows Tom Collins, Oliver Eacott, and Freddie Hook with the engine.

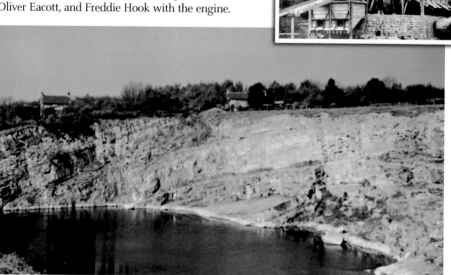

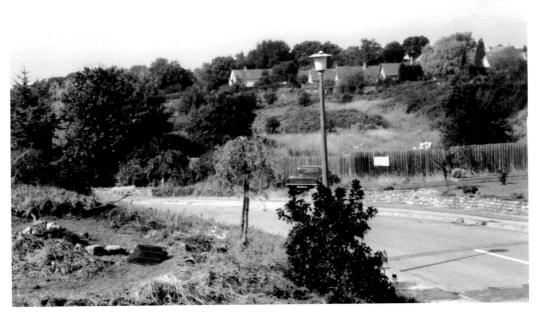

Quarry and Willoughby Close
In the foreground work is in hand on the new Methodist Chapel, a new road has been constructed called Wolfridge Ride, and the Greenhill Quarry has been filled in. Willoughby Close was built on the quarry site in the 1980s.

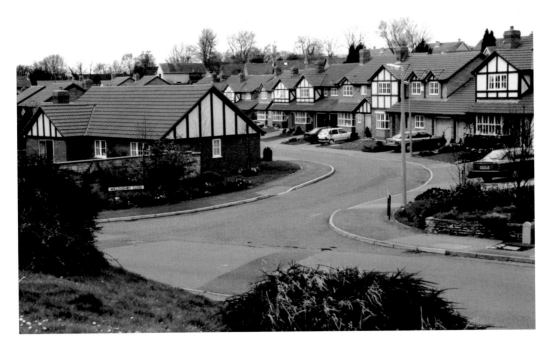

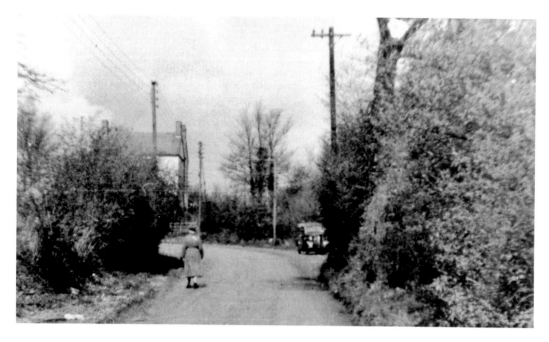

Thornbury Gazette

Extract from the *Thornbury Gazette* 21 March 1959: 'Alveston has a golden opportunity of creating a village centre with half a dozen shops on the edge of a village green near The Bodyce, in view of the projected big development between Down Road and David's Lane'.

Greenhill Road had turned at right angles in front of the new shops, but it was now extended to join Down Road following the line of a former footpath. A section of the old road remains, where one of the village pumps once stood.

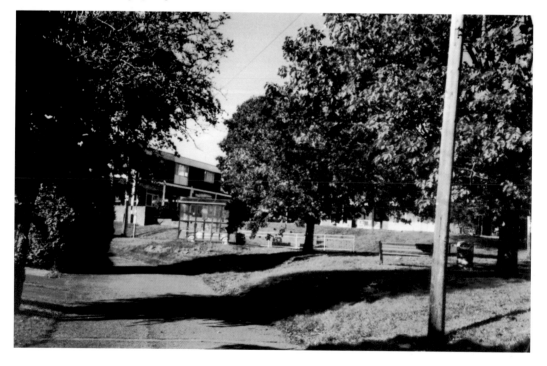

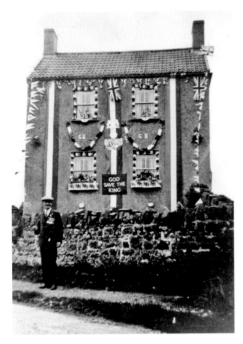

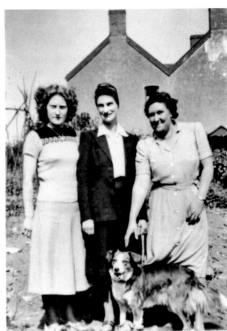

Rock House

(Left) Rock House, a small holding once owned by Mr Moxham and later occupied by Mr Arthur Biddle was demolished and seven shops were built. (Right) Mrs Warren and friends – she and her husband were the last to live in the cottage. (Below) Dancers from the Folk Companions entertain in front of new shops. This picture was taken before the elm trees succumbed to Dutch elm disease.

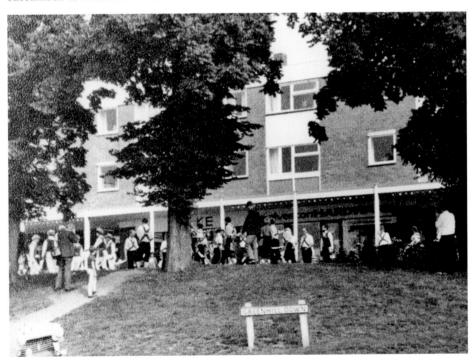

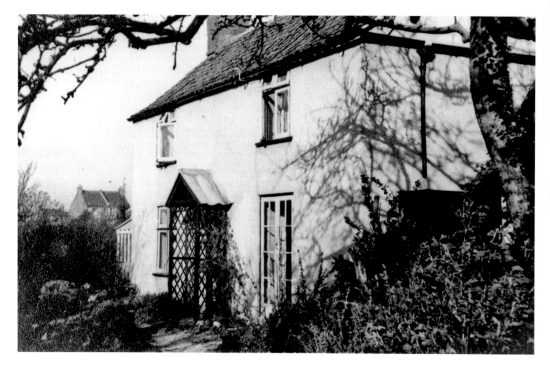

Bodyces Farm

A smallholding owned by the Cullimore family which originally included fields called Upper and Lower Bodyces, and was total of fourteen acres. Over the years, land was given for the Chapel, some was sold for the Greenhill Quarry, and Greenhill Gardens. Mrs Savery sold the orchard for building in 1963. The old farm buildings where Percy Savery had his implement repair business and where people from Bristol slept to avoid the bombing are all now built over.

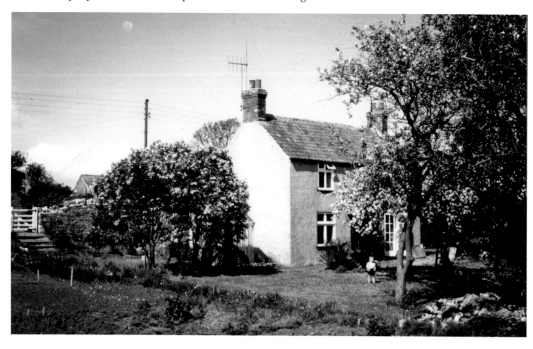

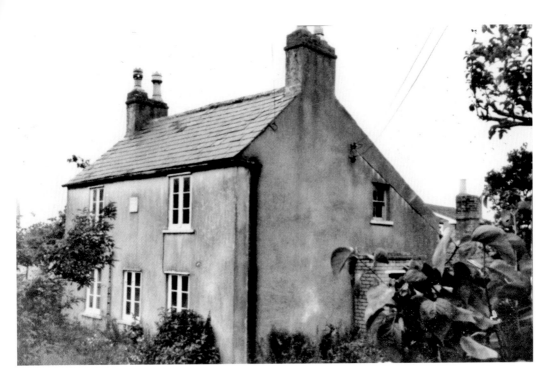

Penrose Cottage

Penrose Cottage built in 1846 by Isaac Ann., and later home to Mr and Mrs Richard James and their children Ruth and David. Richard James was a retired Lieutenant Commander R.N. from Australia, an engineer who worked on H.M.S *Hood*, and on the yacht of King Farouk of Egypt. Ruth emigrated to Australia, and David to Canada.

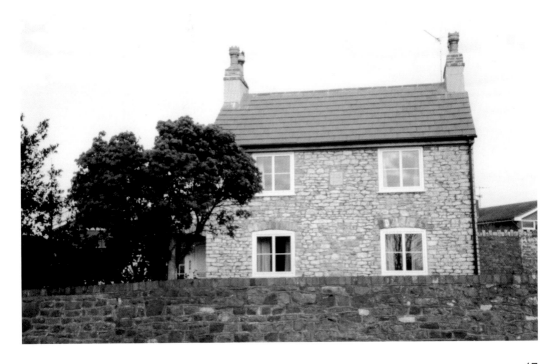

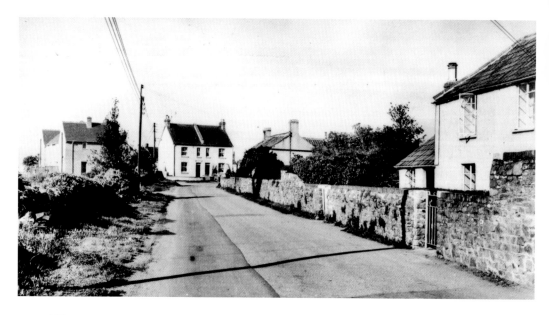

Greenhill Down

(Below, left) Sid Haines, Gordon and Jean fetching water from the village pump in 1934. Many houses had rainwater cisterns in their gardens, but in a dry summer water had to be fetched from the various village pumps or even from the 'dropping well' off the Stroud. (Above) Now named Greenhill Down and pictured in the 1960s. (Below, right) Mrs Tom Collins outside Greenhill Villas, built on the drying ground of the next door laundry.

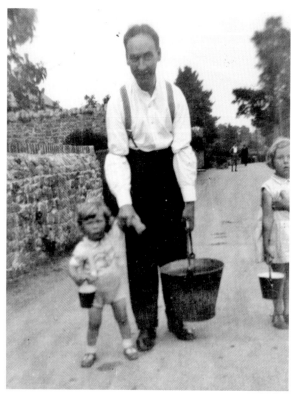

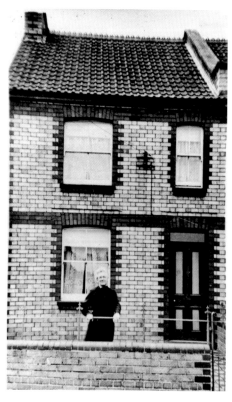

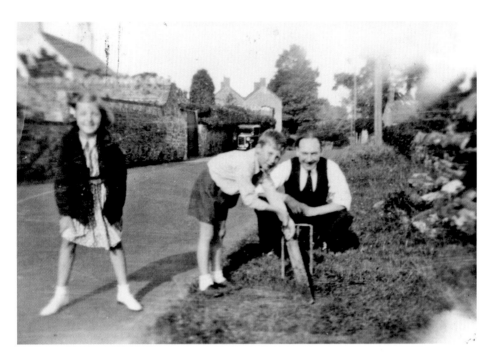

Greenhill Gardens

Playing cricket on the side of the road in about 1939. To the right of the picture was a field which was used by local people as allotment gardens, now Greenhill Gardens estate. Below is Joan Collins at her gate, wife of Gilbert Collins. He was a local bellringer for many years.

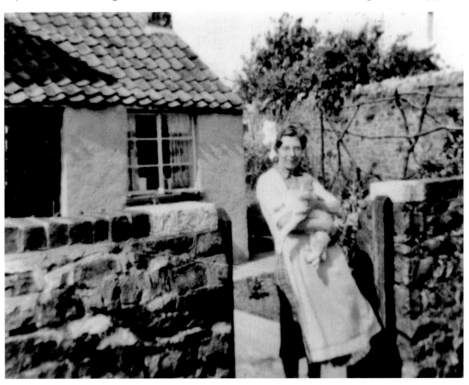

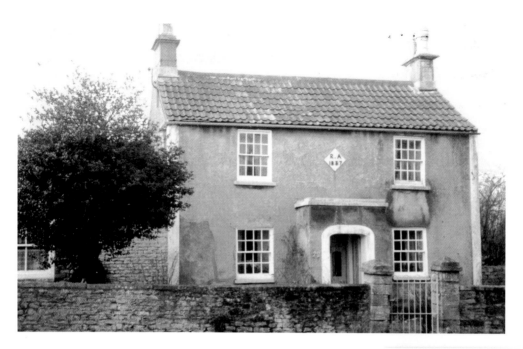

The Hollies

The Hollies date stone says R.A. 1837 for Robert Ann the builder.
It was later occupied by the Boulton family and used as a laundry.
When it was emptied in 1980s the name tapes of Mr Bostock-Smith
who had lived in Davids Lane, and died in 1939 were still on the
window ledge. It was also a carpenter's shop and undertakers.

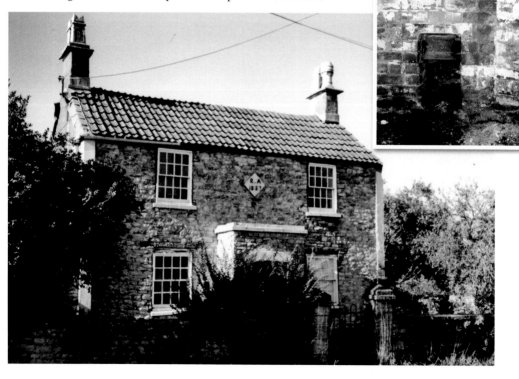

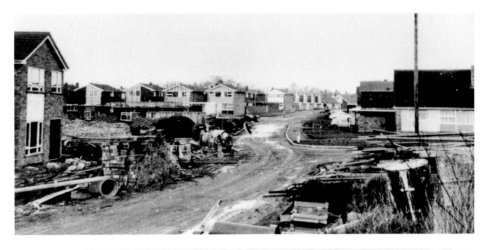

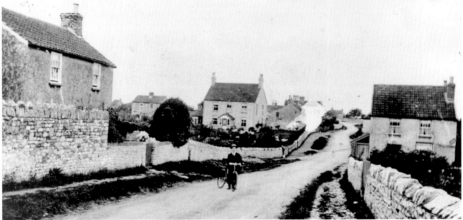

Building Work

The large expansion of the village mentioned in the *Gazette* extract of 1959 (see page 44) started here. A new road meant demolition for the cottage on the right of the middle photograph. The bottom picture shows the house where the Eacotts and daughter Olive O'Neill lived.

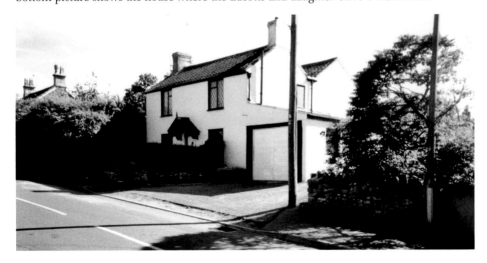

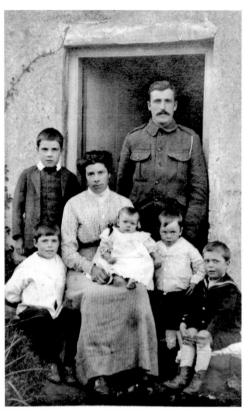 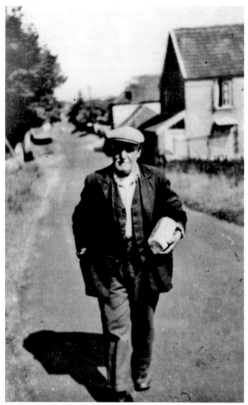

Oliver Eacott

Oliver Eacott son of Rosalinda Chambers and Edgar Eacott, born 1889 and served in the First World War. These pictures show him in uniform with the mule lines in France, and with his family. The baby is daughter Olive O'Neil who lived here later.

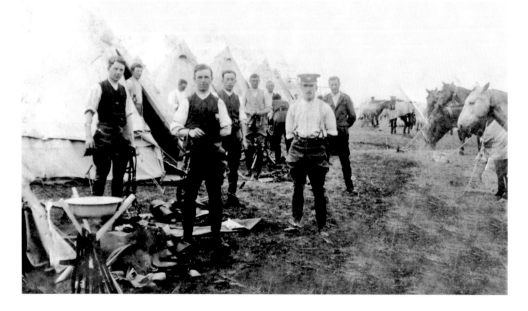

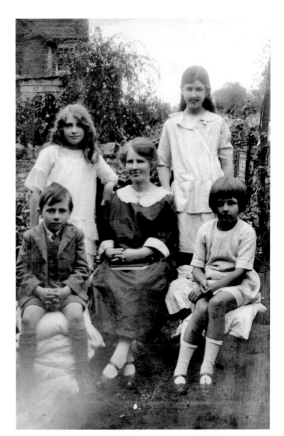

Stanley Chambers

Looking out of The Square, the house on the left was the home of Stanley and Maud Chambers. Stanley was the son of John William Chambers, and grandson of Edward Chambers, all shoemakers. Maud was a school teacher at Thornbury and Tytherington. She is seen here with daughter Helen, Ruth James, John Moxham and Irene Salter in 1926, in a photo headed 'my pupils'. She had a small school for about five years.

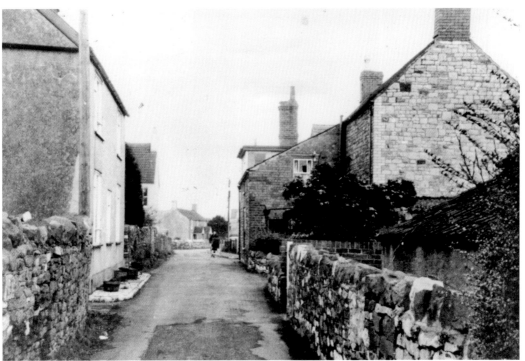

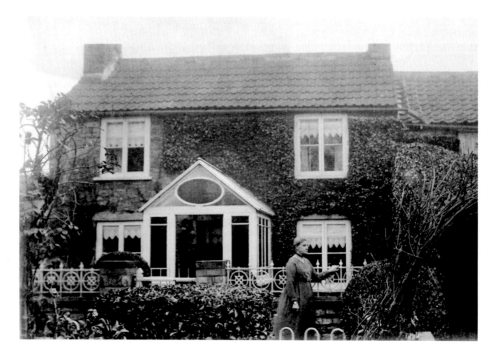

The Pitcher Family's Home

Rhoda Pitcher in the garden of their home on the corner of The Square and Wolfridge Lane. Rhoda and her mother were dressmakers, their workroom now called White Cottage, was made into a house in the 1940s. Several cottages in this area had workrooms attached, which have been incorporated into homes over the years.

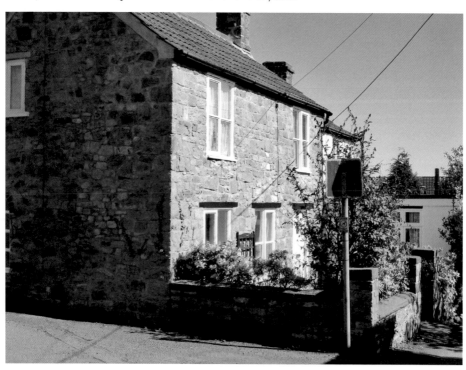

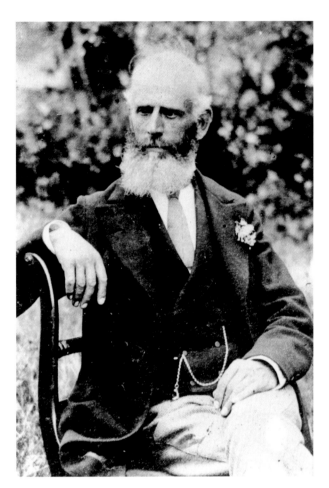

Bloomfield

Bloomfield Pitcher, brother of Rhoda. He is described on the Census as an 'Estate Agent' but this seems to mean 'a collector of rent' at that time. Below is the White Cottage, his mother and sister's workroom.

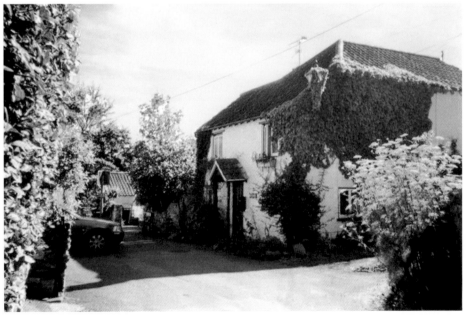

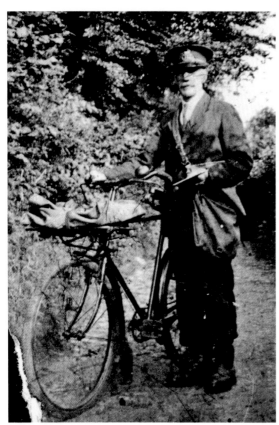

Wolfridge Lane

Wolfridge Lane, was the Saxon boundary of Alveston and Olveston. Here you can see Mr Collins with his postman's bicycle, which was a later addition, as the post was originally delivered on foot, even to the outskirts of the parish at Earthcott and Rudgeway. There were two Collins families living in the lane, but the houses have been replaced over the years and only the stone pigsty of one of the cottages remains. The roof of this cottage was damaged in the war when a plane crashed in the garden. Rumour has it that Mrs Collins was so deaf she didn't hear it!

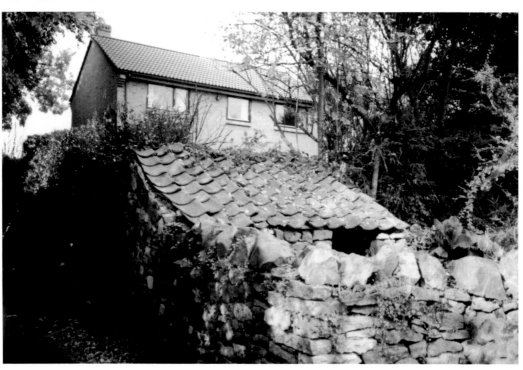

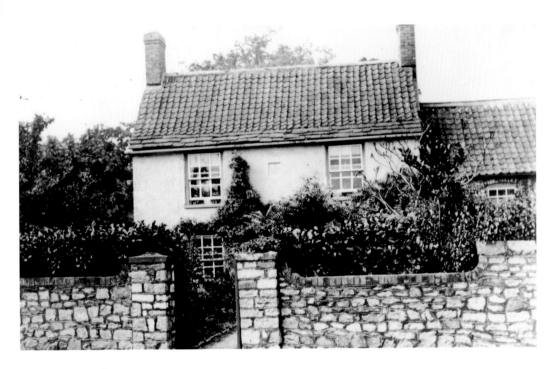

The Laurels

(Above) This was the Liddiatt home, and with its neighbour, they were two of the oldest houses in The Square. The Laurels and house adjoining are both on an 1826 map, and were originally woodsmen cottages belonging to Mr Peach of Olveston. (Below) January 1908 wedding picture of Florence Riddiford daughter of Thomas, and Edgar Liddiatt son of Charles.

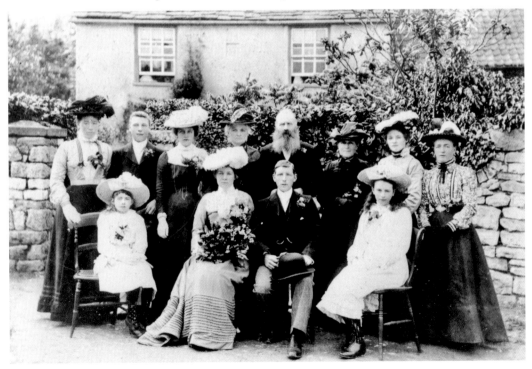

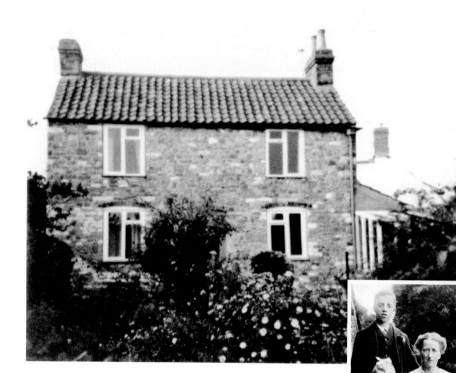

Walter and Amy Biddles Cottage

Walter James Biddle married Amy Melinda Neate in 1903. Walter served on the Italian Front in the First World War, and suffered from shrapnel damage afterwards. Amy complained that it ruined his shirts when the pieces worked their way out. The cottage has been enlarged in recent years.

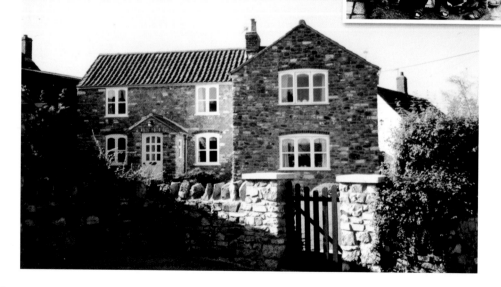

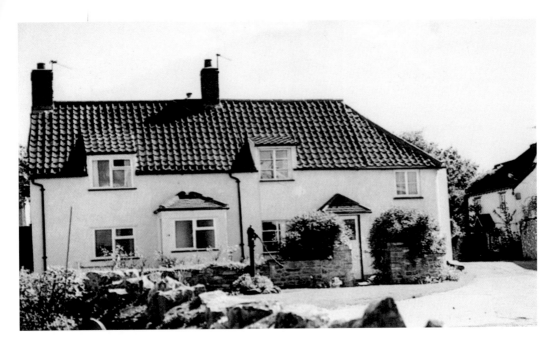

Hares Court and Mayridge

In 1929 the council erected a pump over what had been an open well, and it was not popular at first as it stirred up all the sediment. There has been controversy over the years about the pathway to the well, however it was eventually established as a right of way.

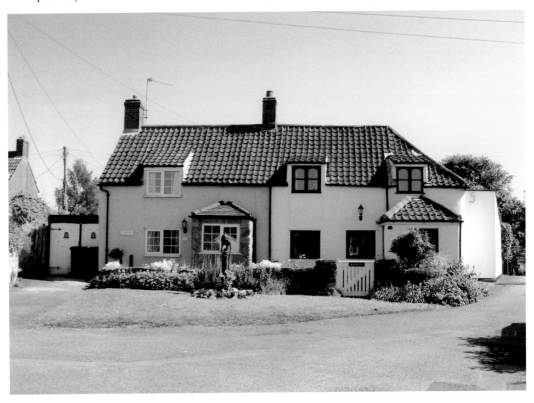

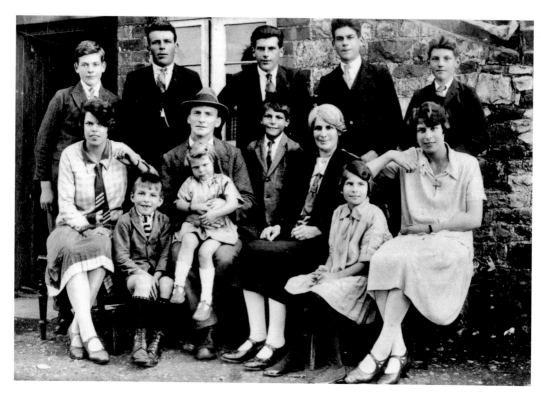

The Baker and his Van

Walter Clark and his family pictured outside their home in The Square. He was the son of William Clark, a blacksmith, originally from Falfield. His relatives continued the craft in The Street, Alveston, although Walter worked for English Bakers, and is shown here with the original baker's van.

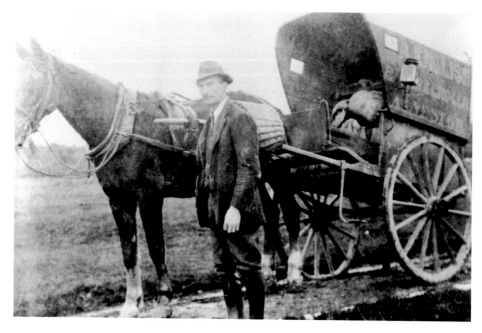

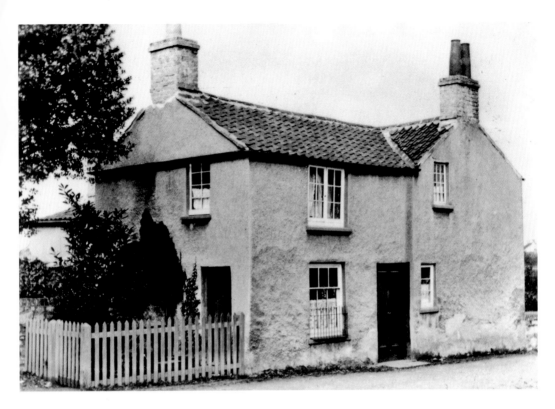

Wye Cottage

Wye Cottage, pictured at the top of the hill into The Square, has now been divided into two houses. When the new Wolfridge Ride estate was built in the 1980s, a road connecting it to both Greenhill Road and The Down had to be constructed. The new road goes through the wall on the right of the picture.

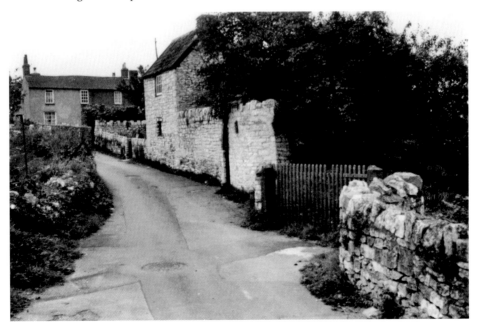

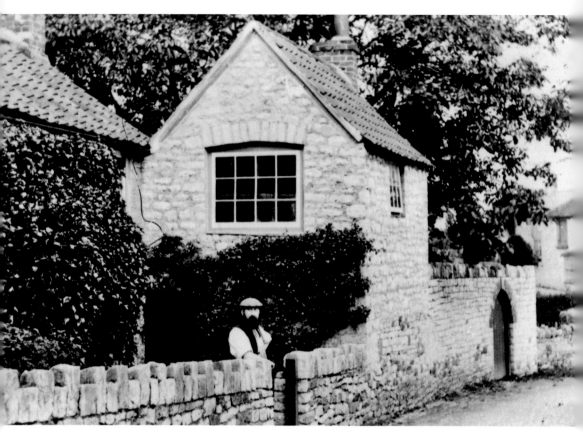

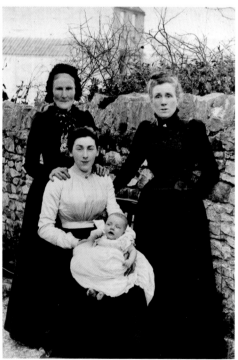

Ivy Cottage
John William Chambers outside Ivy Cottage, with his new two-storey shoe making workshop behind him. Four generations of the family are shown below: John Williams' daughter Charlotte and baby James with her mother and grandmother Wells behind her.

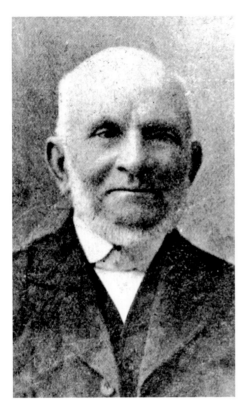
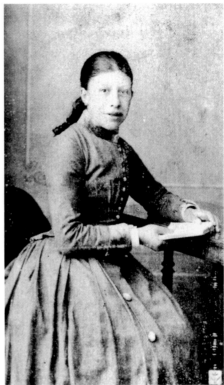

Chapel House

Charles Higgins, baker and butcher of The
Down, was born at Ditcheat, Somerset. He
married Anne Biddle of Oldbury, and was
a staunch Methodist and local lay preacher.
Charles was one of the builders of the
chapel on The Down in 1883, and Chapel
House, where he spent his retirement. He
was also responsible for a new front on the
bakery in 1870.

Charles' wife, Anne, plus their son,
William, are also pictured. There are
still descendants of the family living in
Somerset and Wales.

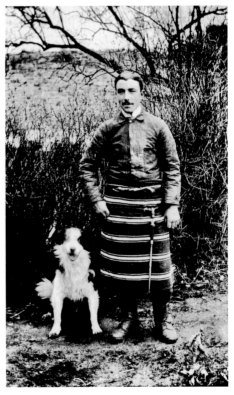

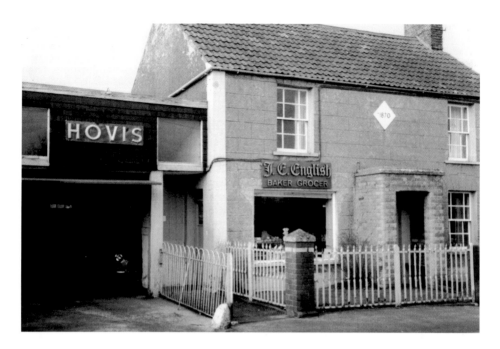

English Bakers

English Bakers took over from Charles Higgins, and they made and delivered bread and groceries all around the Severn Vale. Originally from Malmesbury, the family's first baker's shop opened in Thornbury, and later, another one in Alveston when Arthur English came to join his brother. Arthur had three sons, Frank, Charles and Jack. The picture below is of Jack's marriage to Dorothy Uphill. They had no children, and it was Charles' sons, Frank and Brian, and later Brian's wife, Jenny, who continued to run the business until it closed in 1984.

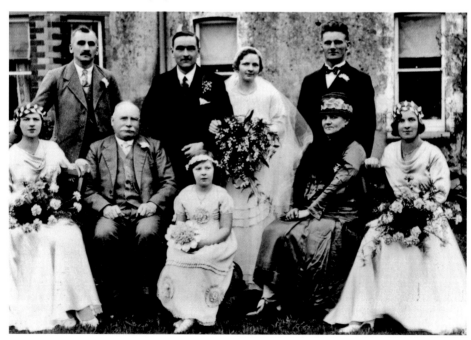

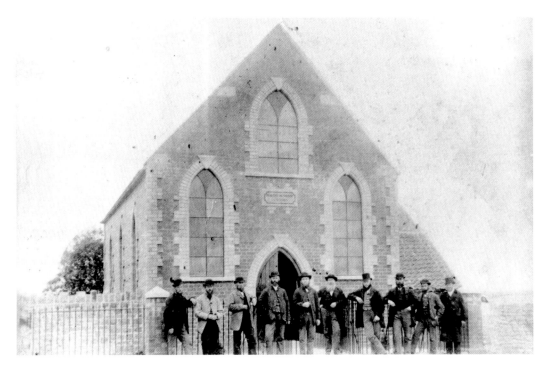

The Chapel and Builders

The builders, including Charles Higgins and Henry Hadrell, completed the chapel in 1883. It replaced the small chapel built by James Lackington, a London bookseller, on the opposite side of the road. James bought two estates in Alveston in 1795. The chapel was converted into a house in 1992. The site of the original chapel is now a small graveyard where Charles Higgins, his wife Anne and son Frederick, who died in a riding accident, are now buried.

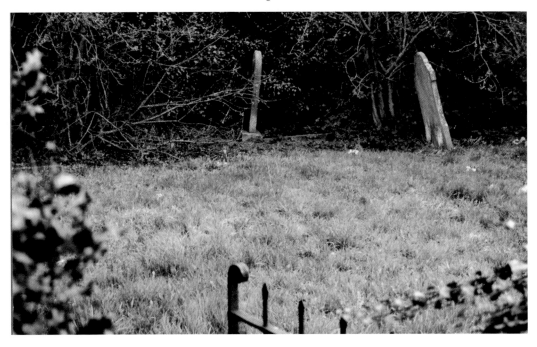

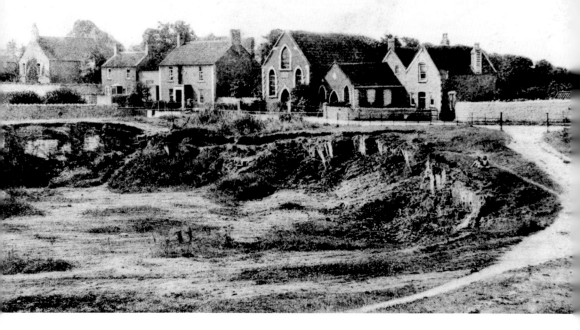

Alveston Quarries

Alveston had many quarries over the years; the Saxon charter refers to Wolfridge, Greenhill and Man's Daele or Quarry. Opposite the Cross Hands there were two quarries; one owned by the Turnpike Trust, and the Village Quarry, where local people could collect stone. There was a ridge of stone between the two quarries. This view shows the remains of the Turnpike Quarry, and the Chapel, and Chapel House in the background. In 2009 the quarry is now a playing field.

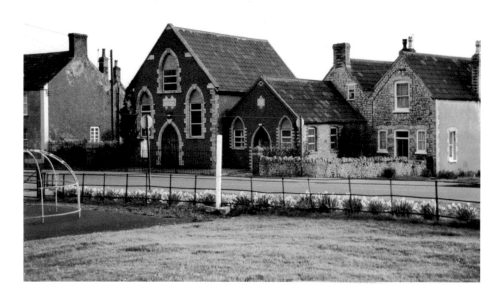

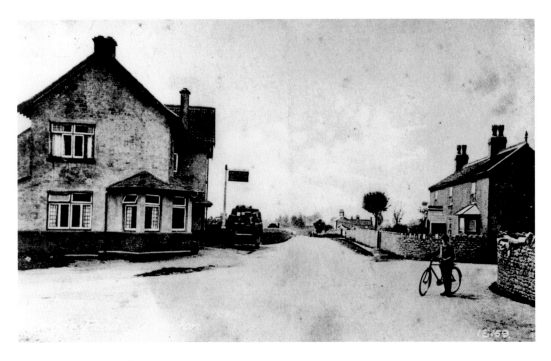

The Cross Hands

From 1871 the Cross Hands was listed as a Beerhouse. William Stephens and his wife Charlotte lived there, and were joined by James T. Neate who ran the new extension. These views in about 1920 show the newer building. James emigrated to America with a friend George Alway. George's sister, Hannah, and Tracy Smith also went to America and the two couples married, although both later returned to Alveston. James William Neate, the son of James T. and Hannah, was born in America.

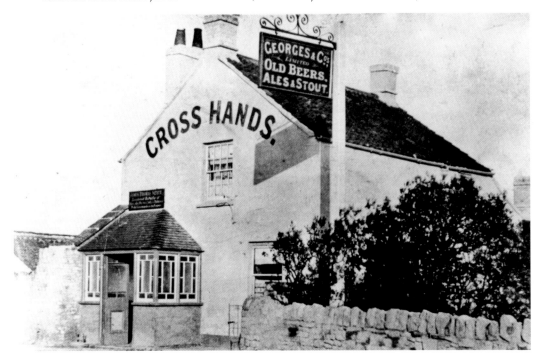

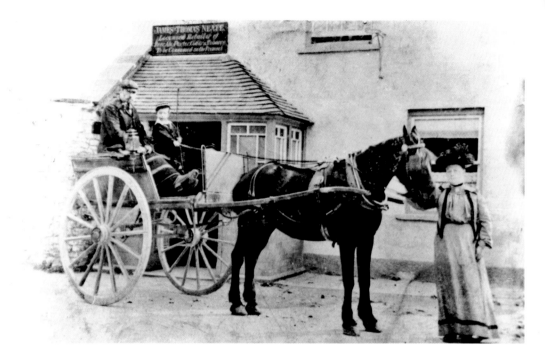

James Neate

(Above) James W. Neate and his wife the former Kate Vizard, with their son William, all in their time licencees of the Cross Hands. William married in 1931, and his wife May continued as landlady until the 1990s. (Below) Coach outings started from the Cross Hands; despite solid tyres and and open top they were known to go as far as Snowdon for the day. This one was heading to Weymouth in 1927, with Mr and Mrs Tom Collins and Mr and Mrs Henry Haddrell in the front seats.

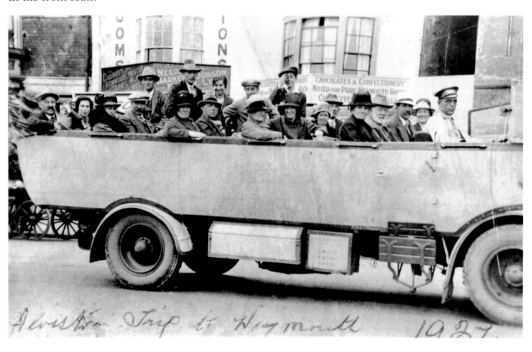

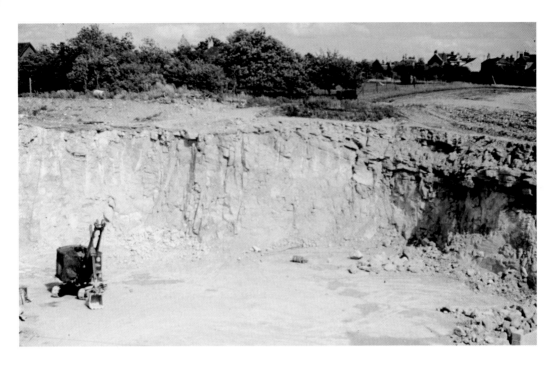

Digger in the Quarry

To the south of the Cross Hands was another quarry, probably started by Charles Higgins. It was taken over by Gloucestershire County Council after his death, and then run by the Curtis family until the 1970s. Although no quarrying took place at this date concrete blocks were made. The quarry was filled in and part of Lime Grove built, and Bush Court added at a later date.

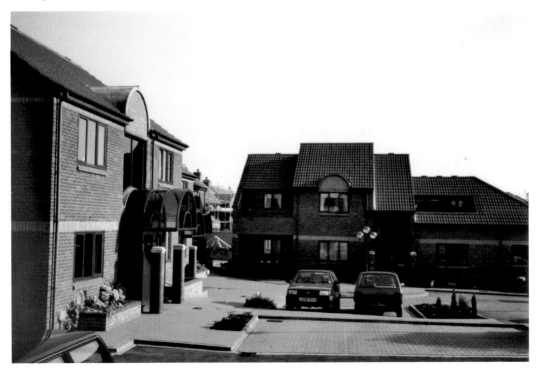

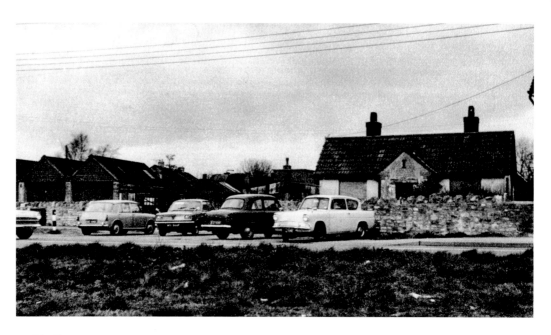

Haddrell Court

Haddrell Court, named after one of the first lady Parish Councillors Margaret Haddrell, was built on the site of the old Gloucestershire County Council Highways Yard. It is pictured here ready for demolition in 1974. Originally Hadrell Court had a flat roof but this was replaced. To the north of these buildings was the old workhouse, later a farmhouse where the Paynes family lived, and now part of the Quarry Mead Estate.

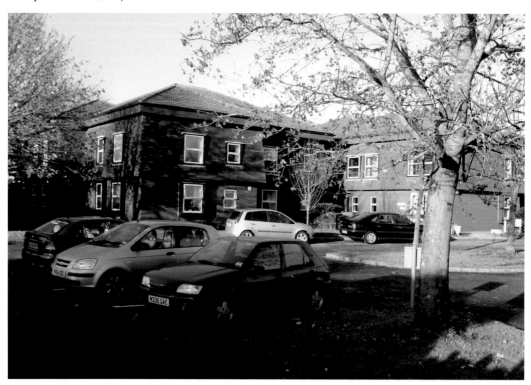

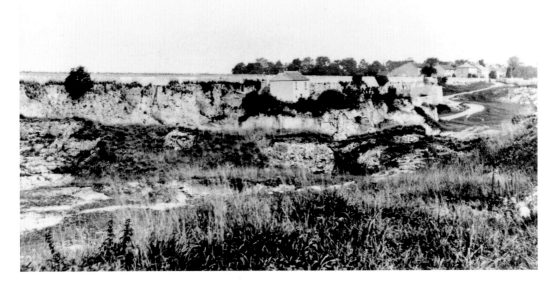

Twenty One Steps

Between the two quarries on Down Road there was a house called Twenty One Steps, or earlier Quarry Cottage, when it was sold in 1940 with 'a partly worked limestone quarry of two acres' formerly the estate of Mr C. J. Moxham. The quarries were filled from 1938 until the mid-1950s and the house was eventually demolished. Filling the quarry caused many complaints to the Council because of the smell, flies and insects, but the resulting playing field was probably worth it!

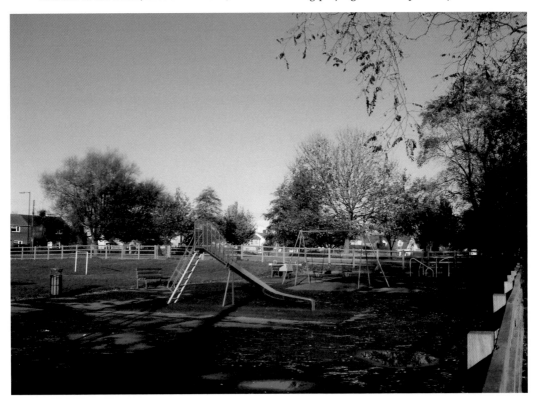

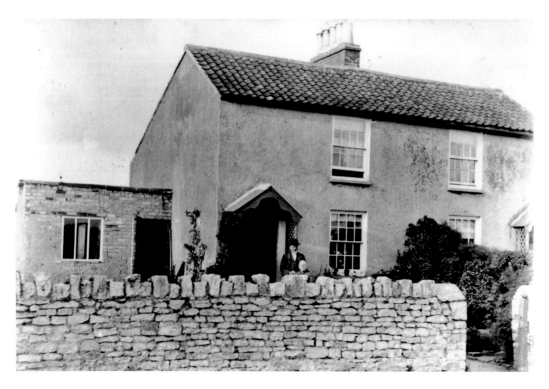

Down Road

An 1827 map shows Down Road as a track across a large common, these houses were built after the 1840 Enclosure Act, when the wasteland on the sides of the road was allocated to various owners of adjacent land in one acre plots. The present shop has been extended over the years as has Rose Cottage next door.

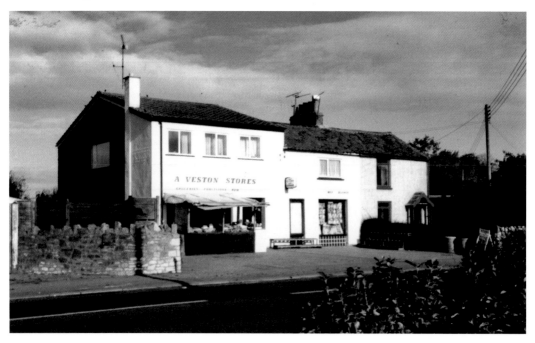

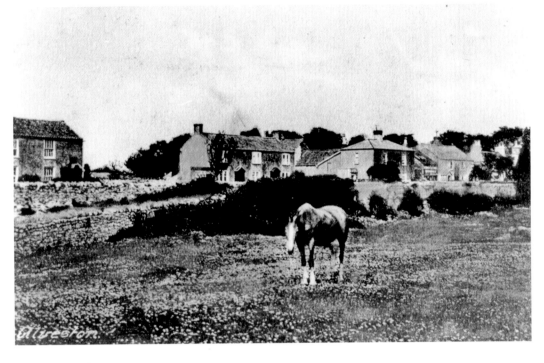

Barton Cottage

(Above) Down Road in the 1920s. Barton Cottage in the centre with Porch House to its right.
(Below) Barton Cottage, originally two houses, was made into one house by Miss Cook, a teacher from Thornbury Grammar School in about 1950. In the 1980s it was demolished and three houses were built on the site, now called Barton Close.

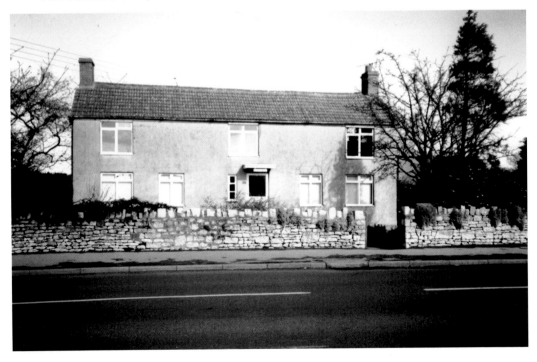

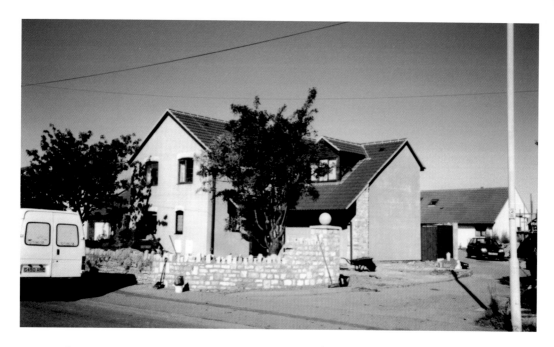

Barton Close and School at Porch House

One of the new houses built at the entrance of Barton Close after the demolition of Barton Cottage. Mrs Emma Webb on the right of the picture had a school at Porch House for a number of years – the Dame schools prospered even though the school at Rudgeway had opened in 1836. Emma was the daughter of Mark Ann who kept the post office on the A38. The picture dates from 1898 judging by the age of Margaret Moxham (Haddrell) fourth from the right in the front row.

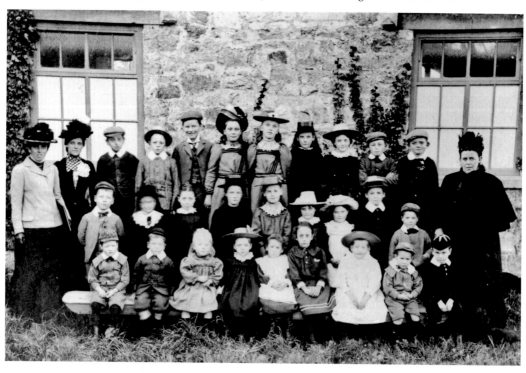

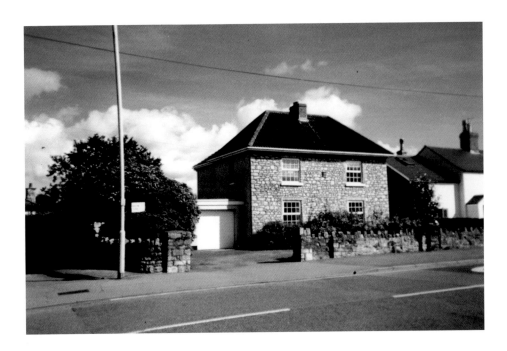

Porch House

Mark Williams Carpenter & Wheelwright and later the home of Sidney and Emma Webb. Emma had a school here for a number of years, from the age of twelve she played the harmonium in the old church at Rudgeway. Among the pupils is Margaret Haddrell, formerly Moxham, and Elsie Burgess. Another pupil was Harry Grindell Matthews, about whom a new book had just been published called *The Death Ray Man*. Harry was born in Winterbourne and attended the school in 1888. The school room on the rear of Porch House has now been made into a living room.

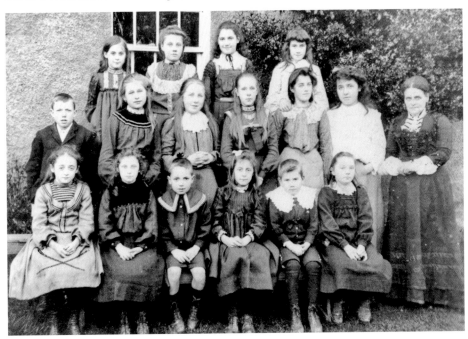

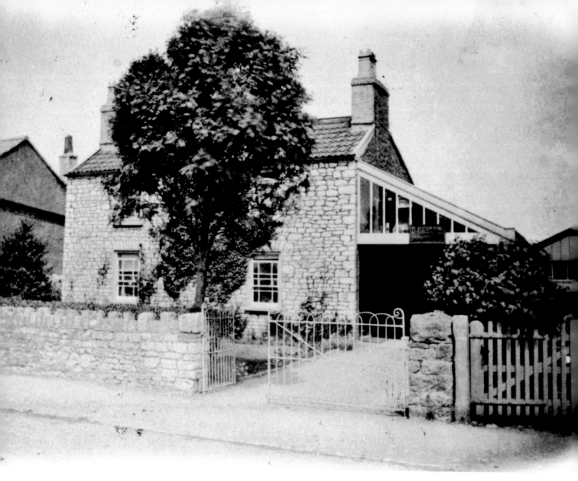

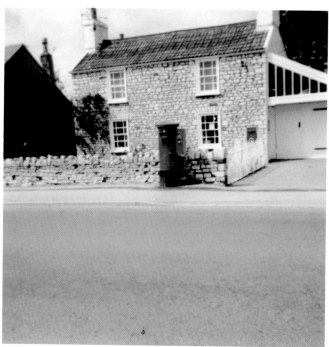

Down Road and Post Office
Former Post Office and home of Robert Parker Curtis and his daughter Elsie Burgess. Robert was a plumber who took on the job of sub postmaster in 1908. In early days the post arrived from Charfield by horse and cart at 5.50 am, and the last mail left Alveston for Bristol at 8pm. Mrs Burgess retired in 1971 after over sixty years, and the post office was moved to the newly-built shop on Greenhill Parade.

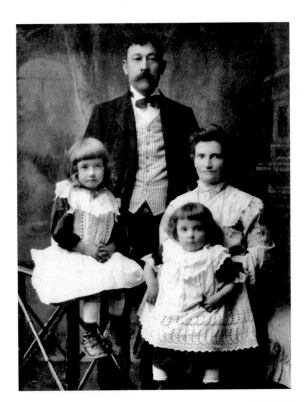

James Collins
James Collins and his wife the former Mary Jane Bell and their daughters Rose and Ivy, who married Frederick Grove. James worked at the Steadings for many years. Pictured here with his employer, there was apparently a large aviary in the garden.

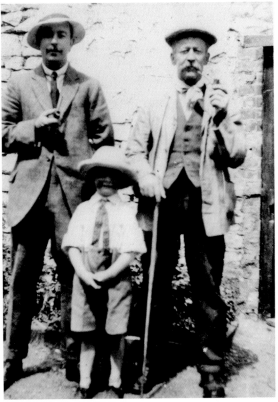

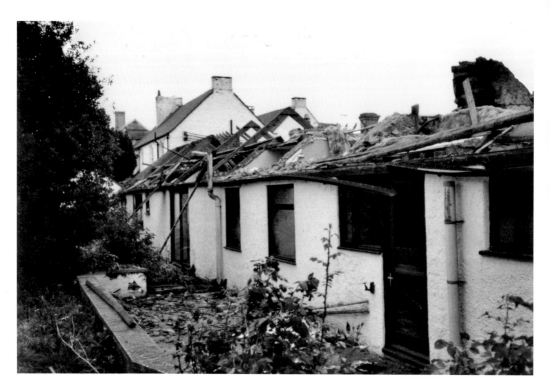

The Berkeley Hunt

Formerly stables and part of the Ship Hotel, the Berkeley Hunt brought the hounds to Alveston once a year while their kennels at Berkeley were cleaned. The stables were then made into a bungalow called The Steadings. This has since been demolished and two new houses built on the site.

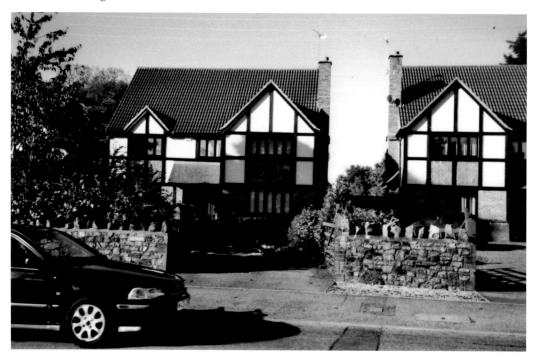

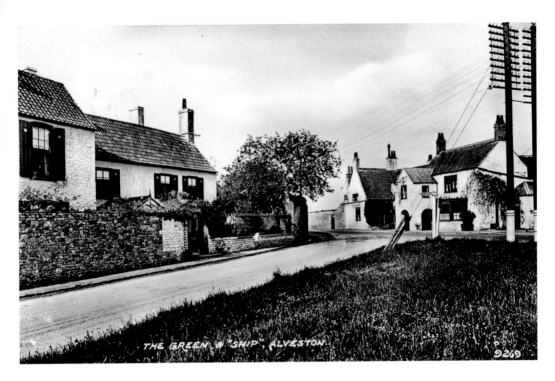

The Old Farmhouse

The Firs and adjoining Forecastle were once one house. Sale particulars of 1920 refer to The Old Farmhouse. John Salmon, former Mayor of Thornbury died here in 1800, his grandson also John Salmon lived here until his death in the 1840s. It was later home to Samuel Stutchbury, whose sister married E. M. Grace the Thornbury Doctor and Coroner. Samuel was born in Demerara in 1844, he bought Bodyces Farm, and established Greenhill Quarry on part of the land. The houses look very different in the 1950s when the green was being dug up.

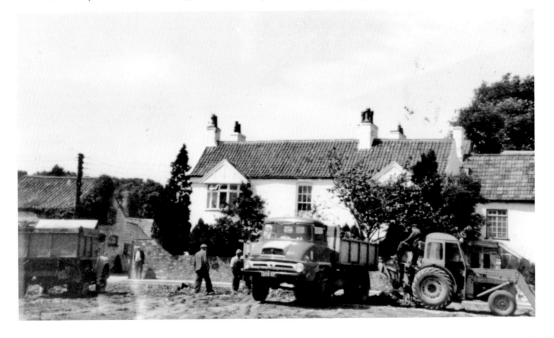

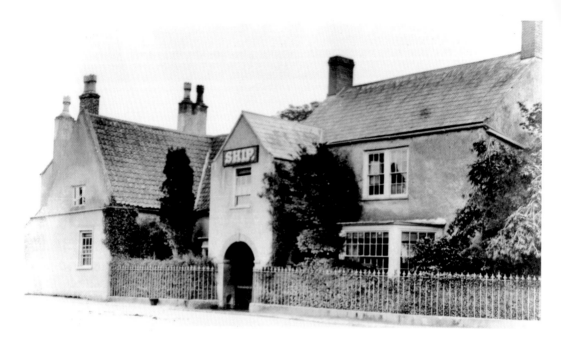

The Ship Hotel

The house now known as the Ship Hotel has origins back to the sixteenth century. It was home for 100 years to the Doward family who were innkeepers in Thornbury and Alveston. Ralph Bigland in his *Gloucestershire Collections* says 'an Inn known by the sign of The Ship has lately been fitted up in a commodious manner for the convenience of travellers'. Originally a farm with forty acres of land, the premises were acquired by Trust Houses in 1912. Over the years the Ship was used for many meetings. Edward Jenner and his friends had a 'Convivio Medico' Society, local landowners met to discuss problems with tenants, village feasts were held here before the Jubilee Hall was built, and wedding receptions in the Tudor Room until the 1950s when the rear of the hotel was rebuilt as a motel.

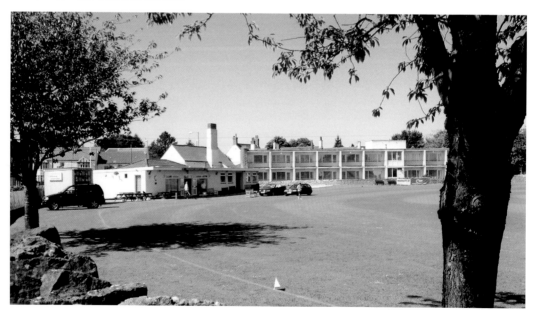

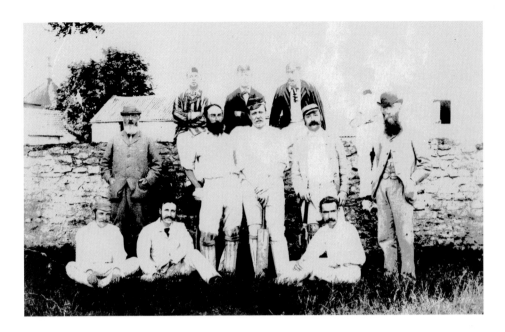

Cricket in Thornbury and Alveston

Thornbury Cricket Club was formed in 1851, and in 1872 it moved to Alveston, to the field next to the Ship, and they've played there ever since. This early photograph shows E. M. Grace with the bat and Mr Chambers as umpire. W. G. Grace, Edward's brother, and Edward's son Edgar, another Thornbury doctor, played here many times. The second photograph shows the Alveston teams when they were promotion winners in 1988. A separate club was founded in 1953, their home field being the recreation ground at the Jubilee Hall. They now have two junior teams and a senior section.

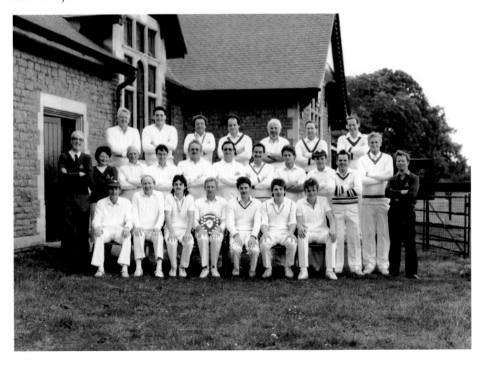

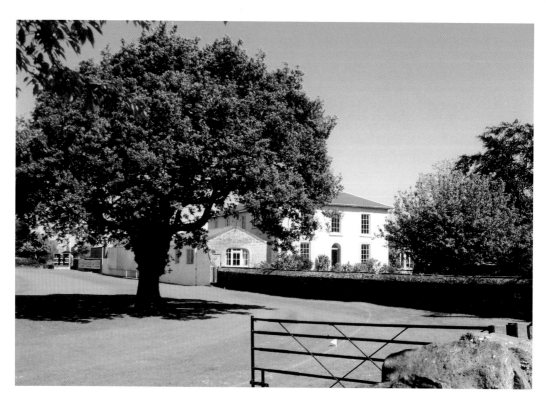

Crossways House

Crossways House was built for the Hopkins family who were coach builders. The large window openings on either side led into the workshops. It was bought by Mr Chester Masters of Almondsbury, and then the Hawkins family who now have a large Hyundai showroom on the site.

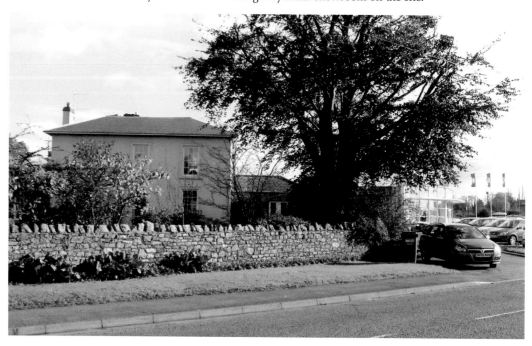

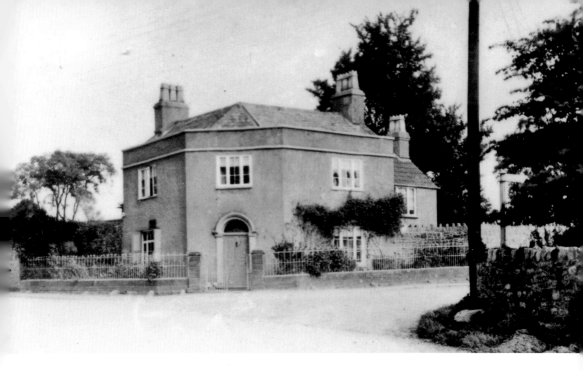

Alveston Post Office

The original Alveston post office was demolished in 1933 when a new road was cut through behind the Berkeley Vale garage and the Ship to join the old Gloucester Road. Many accidents were reputed to have occurred on this corner when stagecoaches came from The Street, and along the old turnpike road from Bristol. Now all that remains is the post box. Mark Ann was the first postmaster, he was followed by his son Stephen, who died in 1907 and Robert Parker Curtis became the new postmaster in Down Road.

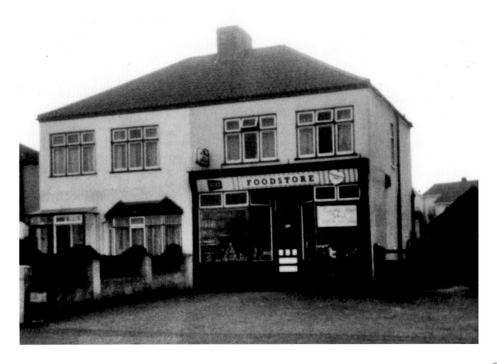

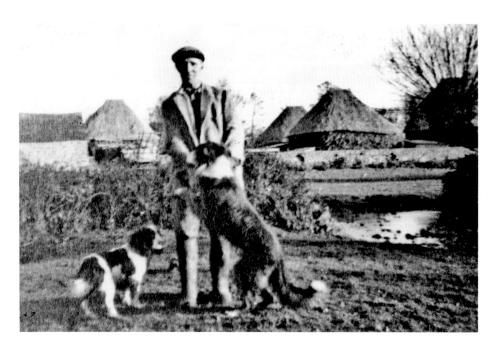

Street Farm

Street Farm has a datestone of 1628. By 1649 a Parliamentary Survey calls the house 'The Manor of the Rectory of Olveston'. It was referred to in this way for many years, and was grouped with other houses and farms in The Street, being leased from the church through an intermediary. In 1802 a valuation remarks that 'the dwelling house Brewhouse and Dairy want considerable repairs, part of the walls of the brewhouse is in danger of falling and the thatched part of the dwelling house is in bad condition'. Over the years the Gunter, Moxham and finally Champion families have farmed here. Robert Champion died here in 2009, and his ancestor John Champion died at Conygre farm in 1809 almost exactly 200 years earlier.

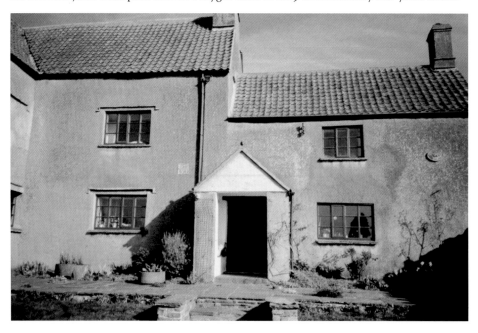

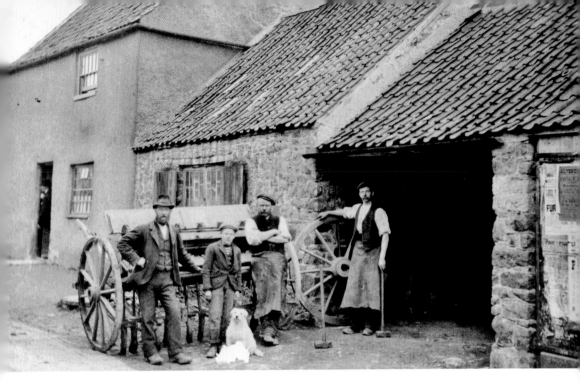

The Blacksmiths

Another house held by copy hold was the blacksmiths, the same survey in 1802 describes it as being 'newly built'. The tenants were Thomas Stephens and his wife Ann who had nine sons. In 1800 Richard was in trouble for receiving stolen goods and was transported to Australia, for fourteen years. The goods came from Mr Helstone's Academy, and the Ship Inn, Alveston. Surviving his journey and sentence, he had a good life in Australia, married and had several children. William another of Thomas' children had a large family several of whom emigrated to Canada, including Edwin, Enos (inset), William, and Clarissa. Esther continued to live in her grandfather's house and had a market garden. This picture is of the Clark family, originally blacksmiths on The Down.

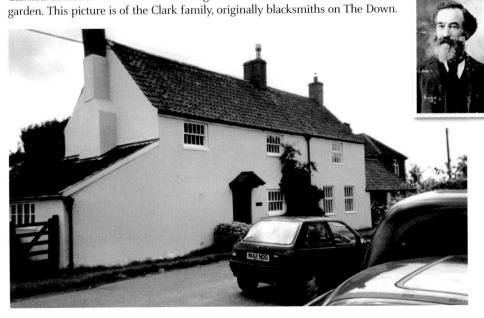

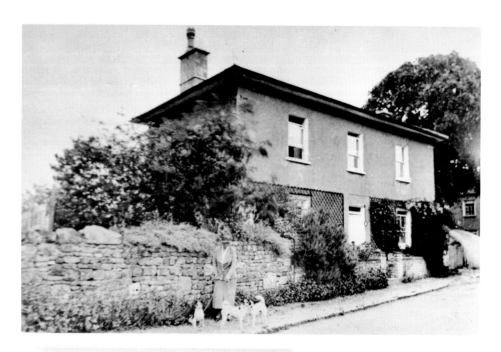

Walnut Cottage

Walnut Cottage had an advertising picture on the wall of an outhouse for Hopkins coach builders. They lived here before building Crossways House. Miss Osborne was a later owner.

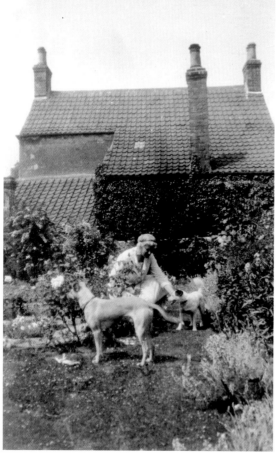

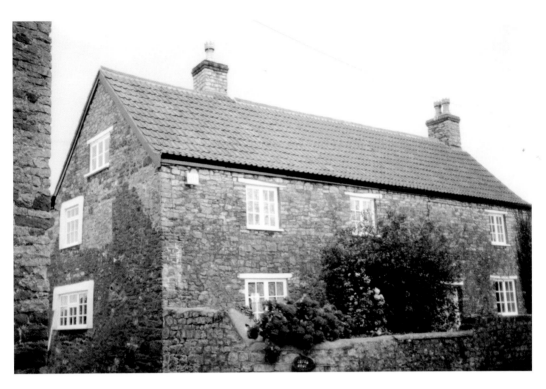

Manor Farm

Manor Farm and part of the original kitchen, also known as Grove Farm, and Home Farm. Henry Haddrell was farm manager here for many years. It was also home to members of the Doward family from the Ship Inn.

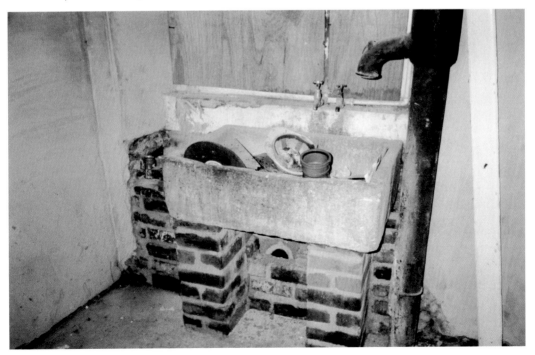

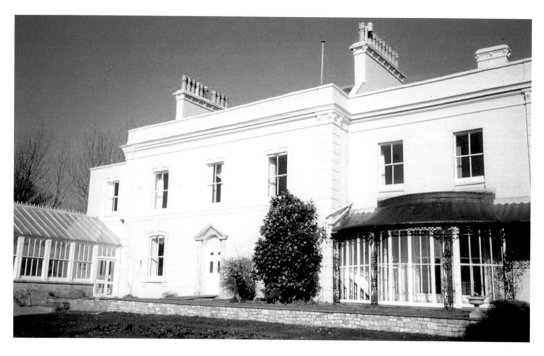

The Grove

The Grove owned by William Bush who married in Alveston in 1813, he inherited the Alveston estate of his mother's family the Whittingtons. His only son died in infancy and his nephew Edward came to live with him as his heir, together with Edward's wife Frances Salmon daughter of John at The Firs. Edward and his brother Thomas were in business as T & E. Bush Engineers, Millwrights, Iron & Brass Founders, Boiler Makers, and Iron Ship Builders of Cheese Lane, Bristol. They built the Brunel Dredger, and pumping engines for Coalpit Heath mines.

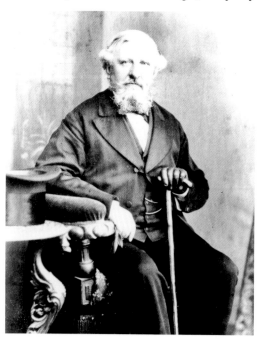

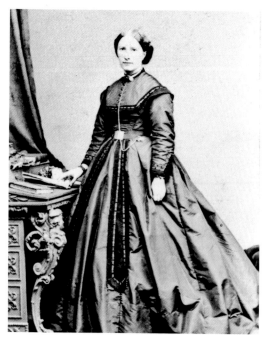

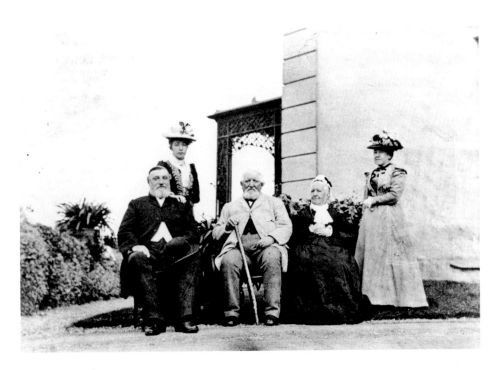

The Bush Family
Edward was chairman of the Bristol Waterworks Co, and director of other firms. He died in 1908. His sisters, Clementina, who never married, and Emily Salmon, a widow, both came to live with him when his wife died. Having no children Henry Graham Bush, Edward's nephew, a solicitor of Bristol – Bush & Bush, Bridge St. – came to live at The Grove. It was later owned by Charles Hill, another Bristol Ship Builder.

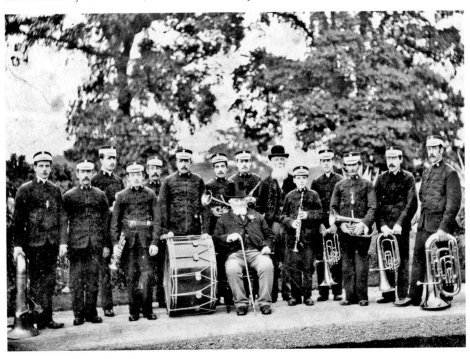

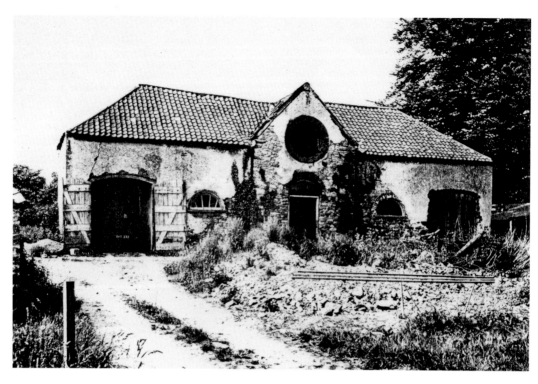

Barn and Stables

Old Alveston House is now three separate properties; the main house, a section at the rear called Dail House, and the barn and stables, now a bungalow, which was converted in the 1980s.

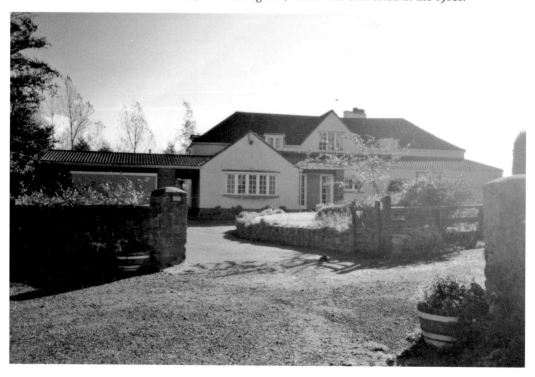

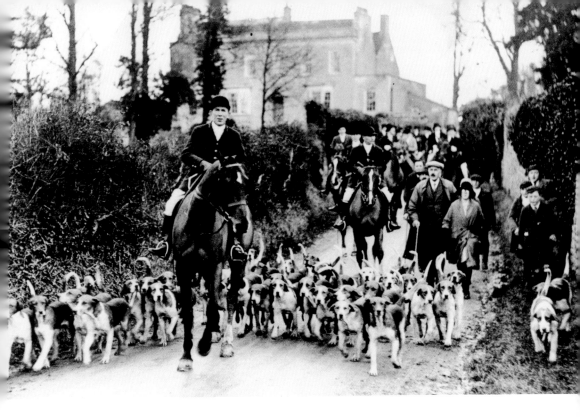

Old Alveston House

Old Alveston House built in the seventeenth century with a new front added in the late eighteenthth century. Henry King a merchant from Bristol bought the house at about this time, he lived here until his death in 1792 with his wife Priscilla. They had two sons, Richard who was a Church of England Rector living in Worthin, Salops, and Henry who carried on the Bristol business of saddlers and ironmongers. Henry didn't marry, and it was Richard's two daughters, Amelia, who married the Revd. John Collinson at Alveston, and Julia, who married Revd. Baker, who inherited his estate. The two Henrys set up the Alveston Charity which was distributed on St.Thomas' Day.

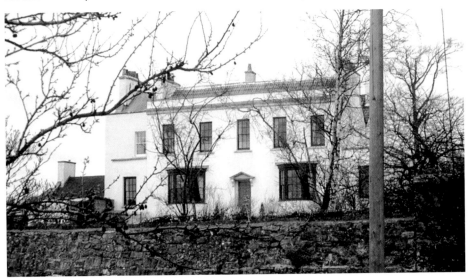

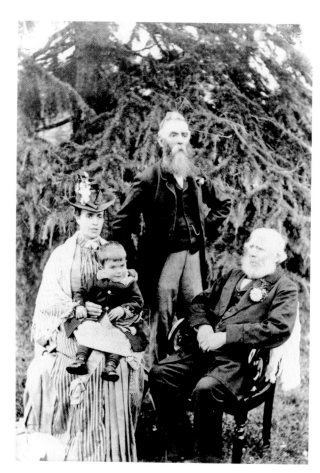

The Chambers Family

Old Alveston House was bought
by William O. Chambers in about
1870. He had run a boarding
school in Wrington, Somerset,
but had trained as a teacher
in Thornbury where he was
born. His grandparents came
from Alveston and the group
photograph shows his daughter
Rosalinda, her son Oliver Eacott,
with William O. and his father,
also named William in about 1890.
The Alveston Brass Band was
founded by William O. Chambers,
and the picture below dates from
around 1900.

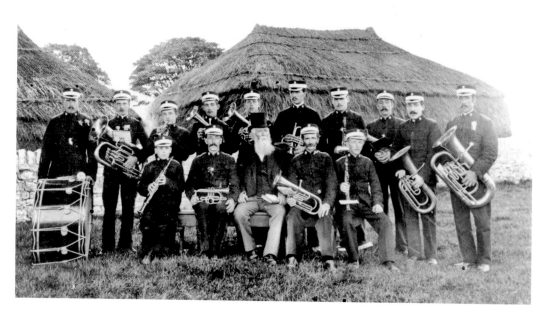

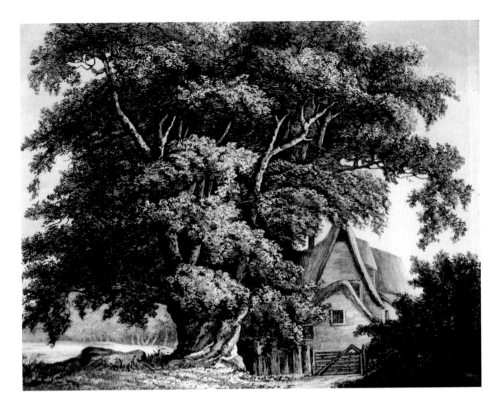

The Alveston Naturalist

One of the people who leased Old Alveston House from about 1813 until his death in 1845 was John Leonard Knapp. He was the author of *The Alveston Naturalist;* the woodcut is copied from the frontispiece of the book published in 1829. The oak tree stood outside what was then called Shelleys Farm, and its occupier Eleanor Haiward – the house is still recognisable under the tree. This was another farm owned by the church and leased through an intermediary. Again a survey of 1802 remarks 'The dwelling house, Barn & Stable want repairing, some of the timber beams under the barn floor and the sills underneath are rotten'. A picture of the tree in about 1890 shows just a skeleton of its former glory, the house, by then had a tiled roof.

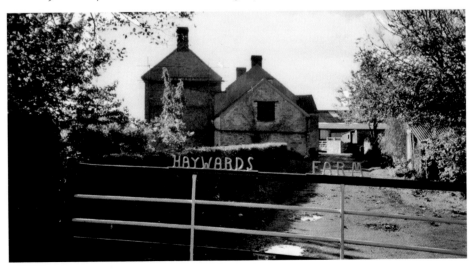

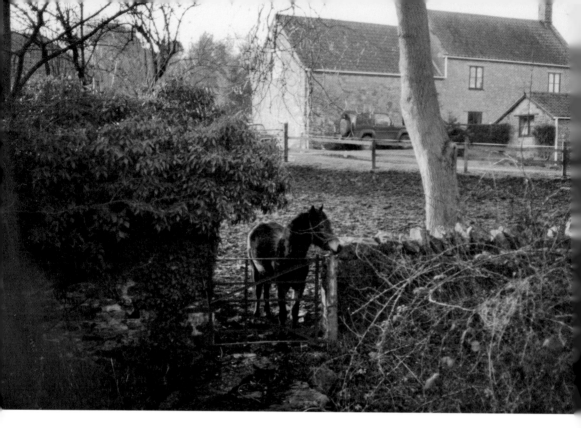

Owls Nest Farm

The photograph below is believed to be of the Champion family, but the Keedwells farmed in Alveston for over fifty years.

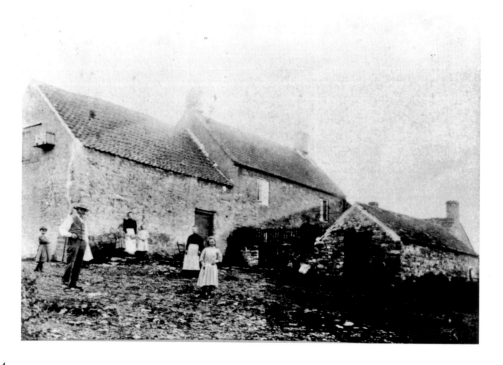

Eliza Wilcox

Eliza Wilcox born in 1804 lived at Conygre Farm from 1809 when her father Robert took over the tenancy on the death of John Champion. Eliza married a Mr Peters at Bitton, had nine children and emigrated to Australia. When her husband died she married again, and came back to live in Wales. Her sister Virtue married Edward Doward. Conygre Farm was sold by Thomas Veel from Alveston Manor in 1646 to pay his fine for supporting the Royalist cause in the Civil War. It was reputed to have been three storeys high when originally built.

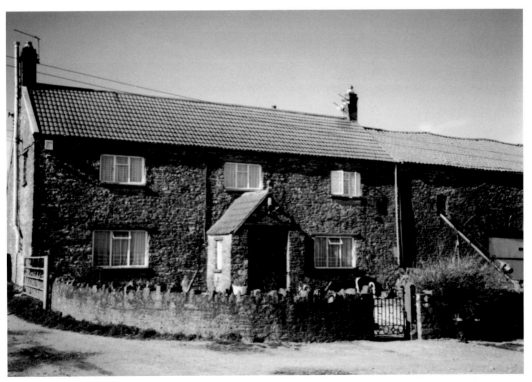

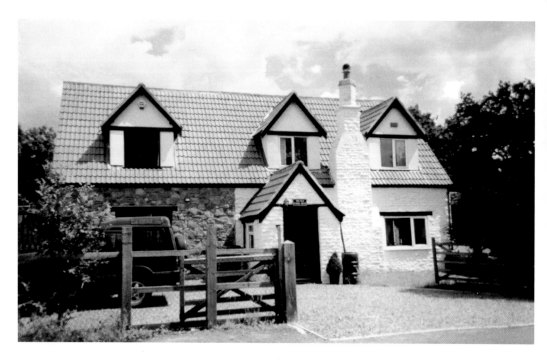

Earthcott School

Earthcott Infants School was built in 1875 so that the younger children would not have so far to walk to the other school at Rudgeway. It had been proposed to build extra classrooms, and a second storey at Rudgeway, this new building was built instead. It closed as a school in 1901 and was only used as a Sunday School when falling numbers made it uneconomic. Later made into a private house, the white painted area was the original school.

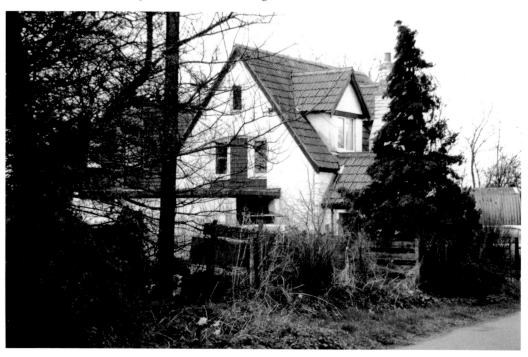